RAGBRAI

AMERICA'S FAVORITE BICYCLE RIDE

GREG BORZO

Charleston   London

THE
History
PRESS

Published by The History Press
Charleston, SC 29403
www.historypress.net

Copyright © 2013 by Greg Borzo
All rights reserved

Front cover, from top to bottom, photographs by: Bob Frank, Dave McWhinnie and Ken Urban.

Unless otherwise noted, photographs are taken by the author or are from the author's collection.

First published 2013

Manufactured in the United States

ISBN 978.1.60949.700.2

Library of Congress CIP data applied for.

I dedicate this book to my daughter,
Roxanne Alice Borzo Bertrand,
who has discovered so many of life's pleasures
—including bicycling—
and is sure to discover many more.

"Hey, is this Heaven?" "No, it's Iowa." These famous lines from the movie *Field of Dreams* are frequently quoted as RAGBRAI rolls through the beautiful Iowa countryside. *Photo by Bob Frank.*

CONTENTS

FOREWORD

What The Great Six-Day Bike Trip Across Iowa [as the first RAGBRAI was called]
is really all about is youth—a state of mind, not an age.

John Karras wrote these words in 1973 at the age of forty-two. Forty-one years later, when he wrote this foreword, he was still maintaining his youthful spirit and participating in RAGBRAI.

⋯⋯

You are holding a comprehensive examination of an annual event of considerable magnitude that Donald Kaul and I started in 1973 in complete innocence of any expectation of what it would become. It's called (I named it, actually) the *Register's* Annual Great Bicycle Ride Across Iowa, RAGBRAI, followed by a Roman numeral designating its order. We're at RAGBRAI XLI this year, and still counting.

The event has evolved, and continues to evolve, since its humble beginning. The truth is that what Kaul and I envisioned was a weeklong ride by just the two of us with the *Register* picking up our expenses. Then the managing editor of the day, Ed Heins, suggested that I "invite the readers to come along," as he put it. I wrote about eight inches of type outlining our intentions, starting point and a few sketchy details of what to expect. (Truth is, I hadn't the foggiest notion of what to expect.)

Opposite: Maintaining traditions. John Karras (right) and Carter LeBeau have tried to share a slice of watermelon on every RAGBRAI. *Kaye and Carter LeBeau.*

FOREWORD

Kaul and I didn't expect anyone to show up and thus were astonished to see 250 or so people in the parking lot at the Sioux City motel we were starting from. So much for our pleasant little solitary romp through the countryside.

From that beginning, participation soared year after year. Astonishing as it is, for all these years it has worked. Hardly any of our worst fears have materialized.

In this book, Greg Borzo has attempted (and in my view succeeded) to capture both the details and the spirit of this grand annual event—an Iowa State Fair on wheels, if there ever was one.

JOHN KARRAS
March 2013

IT'S NOT *JUST* ABOUT THE BIKE

I wish I had gone on the first RAGBRAI, but I had to work that summer. As a taxi driver with the Ruan Cab Company in Des Moines, I remember a few traffic tie-ups when RAGBRAI came through town in 1973. I have a stronger recollection, however, of finding the idea of biking across Iowa in the summer heat with a bunch of strangers a bit crazy. Nevertheless, I was intrigued by the physical challenge that the ride presented. I upgraded to a ten-speed and began to explore road biking.

Back in school at Grinnell College that fall, I decided to test my wings and biked home to Des Moines. The best part of the fifty-four-mile trip was the disbelief from family and friends who couldn't believe I had cycled that far. They were full of questions about the ride—mostly, why?

Such was the state of road biking in Iowa in 1973. People were unfamiliar with, but curious about, this new activity. But I was hooked, and RAGBRAI had planted the seed—as it has done for hundreds of thousands of other cyclists.

RAGBRAI is not *just* about the bike, however. It's a multifaceted gem that engages and reflects many different types and groups of people. Cooks and cops, musicians and ministers, mechanics and mayors, librarians and revelers, as well as cyclists, all have their own take on this weeklong carnival on wheels. Together, they make Iowa go topsy-turvy once a year, celebrating bicycling, food and drink, history, music, culture and small-town hospitality.

Launched as a lark, RAGBRAI survived a carefree childhood, learned lots of lessons through adolescence and is now a mature forty-year-old. RAGBRAI is appealing because, in a society dominated by passive entertainment, it engages people to do something rather than watching others do something. And in a society fixated with sophisticated gadgetry, video games, smart phones, automobiles and urban culture, RAGBRAI revolves around a humble, human-powered vehicle and celebrates small-town culture.

A wet welcome. *Ken Urban Photography.*

Opposite, top: A classical welcome.

Opposite, bottom: A refreshing welcome. *Janet Kersey Kowal.*

RAGBRAI challenges with its own version of a 4-H Club: heat, hills, humidity and headwinds. Such a difficult challenge is unusual in our climate-controlled, couch-potato culture. Through this event, many people—workers and volunteers, as well as cyclists—learn that they are capable of much more, physically and mentally, than they thought.

For cyclists, RAGBRAI is also appealing because it's simple. "The beauty is that all you have to do each day is ride your bike," says Patrick McBriarty, experienced cyclist and author of *Chicago River Bridges*. How refreshing to just pedal; explore the countryside; taste an ear of sweet corn that was picked minutes earlier; share a beer, or two, with friends; be kind to strangers.

And all of this in an unlikely place—a state incorrectly thought of as flat, bland and unappealing.

Whether you brake for libraries or dancing, food or history, bungee jumping or church services, you're likely to find this Iowa showcase, this border-to-border buffet, this small-town extravaganza fun and full of surprises.

Many cyclists visit churches along RAGBRAI, and not only for meatloaf. *Dave McWhinnie.*

Two housekeeping details: All towns are in Iowa, unless indicated otherwise. And "kybo" is Iowan for porta potty. Apparently, it stands for "keep your bowels open," the name of a defunct Iowa porta potty company.

GREG BORZO
reporting from RAGBRAI, Iowa,
the only town in Iowa that stretches across the entire state,
from river to river

ACKNOWLEDGEMENTS

One thing that keeps RAGBRAI, the *Register*'s Annual Great Bicycle Ride Across Iowa, going strong is the incredible number of people who are extremely engaged in the enterprise, have a strong sense of ownership in RAGBRAI and have a profound desire to see it persevere. Many of these veterans stepped up to help me write this book. Their commitment and dedication surprised and impressed me.

Before I started working on this book, Janet Kersey Kowal and John and Sue Becker showed me the generous spirit of RAGBRAI. When I did my first RAGBRAI in 2009, they helped run Team Gourmet, and I couldn't have asked for a better introduction to the ride.

Then in 2012, I had the good fortune of meeting former RAGBRAI co-host Chuck Offenburger. He gave me a great overview and pointed me to umpteen sources. That got the wheels spinning. After that, I met T.J. Juskiewicz, current director, who was extremely supportive and directed me to more vital sources. That got me into high gear.

Several other key players, all of them deeply dedicated to the event, with hundreds of RAGBRAI years between them, helped me understand the true nature of this unique adventure. Heartfelt thanks go to Mike Conklin, Brian Duffy, Jim Green, John Karras, Rich Ketcham, Tim Lane, Kaye and Carter LeBeau, Tammy Pavich, Pete Phillips, Forrest Ridgway and Carl Voss.

Leighton Christiansen, librarian at the Iowa Department of Transportation, was exceptionally helpful in finding resources and answering my questions about Iowa. Elizabeth Adamczyk, librarian at the Northwestern University Library, was extremely accommodating gathering microfilm tapes of old newspapers. Kathy Leonard, librarian at the Des Moines Public Library, helped me track down valuable information. The Drake University Library provided scores of microfilm tapes of old newspapers. The Harold Washington Library Center, my own neighborhood library, provided microfilm reading and digital services. The State

Acknowledgements

Historical Society of Iowa Library shared its large collection of books and files about Iowa and RAGBRAI. And sister-in-law Betty Borzo also helped with my library research.

Rich Ketcham's definitive site, http://geobike.com, was essential to researching this book, and his service to the RAGBRAI community is particularly laudable.

Also, history professor Lisa Ossian at the Des Moines Area Community College was an excellent resource in helping me understand Iowa's history and development, qualities and characteristics. And Andrew Fay was key in connecting me with her.

Although I shot most of the photos in this book, I relied on many amateur photographers to round out the kaleidoscope of images you're now holding. Steve Kobberdahl provided photos from early RAGBRAIs; Janet Kersey Kowal loaned me discs full of photos; Kaye and Carter LeBeau opened their vast collection of images and newspaper clippings; Tammy Pavich and Pete Phillips shared their Pork Belly Ventures' library of photos (shot by Bob Frank); and Dave McWhinnie gave me many photos, in particular aerial shots.

Two professional photographers, Bob Frank and Ken Urban, provided what can only be described as award-winning photographs. (See for yourself at http://www. bafrank.com/ragbrai_links and http://www.kenurbanphotography.com.) In addition, they provided support and leads.

Expert proofreading by Sherry Brenner and John Greenfield, as well as editorial advice from Paul Borzo, greatly improved this book.

And I'm grateful to John Karras for writing the foreword.

Thank you, one and all. Long live RAGBRAI. Now, start your bicycles.

RAGBRAI Vital Statistics

Year	Event	From	To	Event Distance (miles)	Event Climb (feet)	Cumulative Distance (miles)	Cumulative Climb (feet)
1973	I	Sioux City	Davenport	443	17,869	443	17,869
1974	II	Council Bluffs	Dubuque	428	20,687	870	38,556
1975	III	Hawarden	Ft. Madison	464	16,994	1,335	55,550
1976	IV	Sidney	Muscatine	445	19,595	1,780	75,145
1977	V	Onawa	Lansing	379	10,675	2,159	85,820
1978	VI	Sioux City	Clinton	450	16,462	2,609	102,282
1979	VII	Rock Rapids	Burlington	506	15,187	3,115	117,469
1980	VIII	Glenwood	Guttenberg	484	22,579	3,599	140,048
1981	IX	Missouri Valley	Keokuk	505	26,374	4,104	166,422
1982	X	Akron	Davenport	517	16,357	4,621	182,779
1983	XI	Onawa	Dubuque	489	19,791	5,109	202,570
1984	XII	Glenwood	Burlington	472	21,709	5,581	224,279
1985	XIII	Hawarden	Clinton	550	15,648	6,131	239,927
1986	XIV	Council Bluffs	Muscatine	495	22,424	6,627	262,351
1987	XV	Onawa	Guttenberg	451	15,611	7,077	277,962
1988	XVI	Sioux City	Ft. Madison	434	18,304	7,511	296,266
1989	XVII	Glenwood	Bellevue	489	21,855	8,000	318,121
1990	XVIII	Sioux Center	Burlington	496	13,344	8,496	331,465
1991	XIX	Missouri Valley	Bellevue	428	23,162	8,924	354,627
1992	XX	Glenwood	Keokuk	488	24,716	9,412	379,343

Year	Event	From	To	Event		Cumulative	
				Distance (miles)	Climb (feet)	Distance (miles)	Climb (feet)
1993	XXI	Sioux City	Dubuque	536	18,280	9,948	397,623
1994	XXII	Council Bluffs	Clinton	507	23,260	10,455	420,883
1995	XXIII	Onawa	Muscatine	481	18,003	10,937	438,886
1996	XXIV	Sioux Center	Guttenberg	429	14,299	11,365	453,185
1997	XXV	Missouri Valley	Ft. Madison	459	25,369	11,824	478,554
1998	XXVI	Hawarden	Sabula	479	18,495	12,304	497,049
1999	XXVII	Rock Rapids	Bellevue	520	18,318	12,824	515,367
2000	XXVIII	Council Bluffs	Burlington	489	22,885	13,313	538,252
2001	XXIX	Sioux City	Muscatine	517	25,543	13,830	563,795
2002	XXX	Sioux Center	Bellevue	489	15,656	14,317	579,451
2003	XXXI	Glenwood	Ft. Madison	444	23,149	14,761	602,600
2004	XXXII	Onawa	Clinton	487	18,425	15,248	621,025
2005	XXXIII	Le Mars	Guttenberg	484	15,294	15,732	636,319
2006	XXXIV	Sergeant Bluff	Muscatine	444	23,170	16,177	659,489
2007	XXXV	Rock Rapids	Bellevue	479	13,624	16,655	673,113
2008	XXXVI	Missouri Valley	Le Claire	460	21,215	17,115	694,328
2009	XXXVII	Council Bluffs	Burlington	447	23,111	17,562	717,439
2010	XXXVIII	Sioux City	Dubuque	451	14,860	18,013	732,299
2011	XXXIX	Glenwood	Davenport	445	20,371	18,458	752,670
2012	XL	Sioux Center	Clinton	474	16,165	18,933	768,835
2013	XLI	Council Bluffs	Ft. Madison	407	17,410	19,239	786,245

RAGBRAI staff "share the wealth" among different communities across the state, year by year. Kimballton has been a pass-through town the most times (eight), and with RAGBRAI XLI, Council Bluffs will have the most overnight stays (six). *Source: GeoBike.com*

WHY IT WORKS

When I spoke with Tina Castle in 2012, she was twenty-five years old and claimed to have gone on twenty-seven RAGBRAIs! Folks who ride this Mardi Gras on wheels are known for great stories—but also for embellishing those tales. How was Tina going to substantiate hers? It turns out that her mother rode RAGBRAI in 1985 when she was five months pregnant with Tina. The following July, when Tina went on her second RAGBRAI, she wasn't even one year old. And she's been on every RAGBRAI since, first in a support vehicle, then in a trailer, then at the age of four on the back of a tandem and, finally, on her own bike.

Tina and her sister, Becca Olson, grew up in Shenandoah. Their parents, Terry Castle and Karen Garner, started riding RAGBRAI in 1981, fell in love with it and made it their family vacation. They became well known on the ride, Karen for her pigtails and Terry for riding with one arm, having lost the other in a farming accident. "When we were little, we were known as Terry and Karen's kids," Becca says. "Now they're known as Tina and Becca's parents."

Tina has no children, but Becca rode RAGBRAI in 2011 when she was pregnant with her first child. The following year, she took her son on RAGBRAI XL. Therefore, he's off to the same start Tina had: two RAGBRAIs before turning one.

Tina plans to keep riding RAGBRAI as long as possible. "I'd rather do RAGBRAI than go to Hawaii or Cancun, you name it," she says. Living in Washington, D.C., Tina keeps her RAGBRAI bike in Shenandoah—the same set of wheels she's been using for the ride since she was thirteen years old.

—⊷≡✦≡⊶—

The Castle family is not alone in its infatuation with RAGBRAI. This world-famous ride is part of many people's elevator speech about themselves. It's mentioned in

countless obituaries as one of that person's major accomplishments. And it's on the bucket list for an untold multitude.

What is this thing called RAGBRAI? Essentially, it's a weeklong bike ride and festival that combines bicycling, eating, small-town hospitality and partying with family, friends and strangers. In what order these elements are combined depends on the individual. For one, RAGBRAI is a family reunion; for another, it's a beer blast; for yet another, it's a tough test of physical endurance and mental stamina.

Such priorities are reflected in what people call the ride: Woodstock on Wheels, Weeklong Spin Class and Spring Break for Adults. There's also the Ultimate Moveable Feast, That Tootle Across Iowa…and Festival of Nice.

The event is not a wild party—nor is it a Disney experience (except for the long lines).

Some approach RAGBRAI as a pilgrimage. They set out to lose weight or find themselves; give up smoking or sprinkle the ashes of a loved one along the way; conquer an illness or have some fun before an illness conquers them.

I think of RAGBRAI as a cruise, albeit one that requires a bit of exertion from its guests. It offers delicious food, all day long; incredible scenery; first-class entertainment; activities and games; historic stops and tours; the chance to meet tons of people; and exposure to diverse cultures: Dutch and Danish, Amish and Native American and hog farming and Iowana. The rolling hills fill in for the waves, and the bright sun provides suntans (though unconventional ones, due to the cycling attire). And, as on a cruise, Internet connectivity and cellphone coverage are extremely spotty, which takes you out of your daily routine and submerges you into another reality.

Ultimately, the RAGBRAI experience is what you want it to be. The only certainty is that there's nothing else like it anywhere in the world.

RAGBRAI was conceived as a caper without any assurance it would succeed and no notion it would be repeated. Its ponderous name and difficult-to-discern acronym was a joke, to poke fun at America's propensity to create acronyms.

Surprise. The first year worked, and the idea caught on. The first ride attracted a peak of 500 riders, with 114 completing the entire route. Meanwhile, the forty-first ride will likely attract 25,000 cyclists, over the full week, with 10,000 to 12,000 biking

Opposite: RAGBRAI can be a frolic or a pilgrimage, an annual sojourn or the trip of a lifetime. *Ken Urban Photography.*

the entire route. Over those forty-one years, more than one-third of a million spoke spinners will have cycled part or all of the trip.

In forty-one years, RAGBRAI has covered 19,239 miles and climbed 786,245 feet, equivalent to traveling four-fifths the circumference of the earth and climbing Mount Everest twenty-seven times, respectively. In the process, participants have drained rivers of beer and lemonade; devoured jungles of bananas; and delighted in heaps of watermelon, sweet corn and homemade pie.

In the beginning, RAGBRAI was a tough sell to towns along projected routes. Today, more than two hundred communities are on a waiting list to host the event, primarily due to the economic stimulus that RAGBRAI provides. Total direct spending by RAGBRAI in 2010 was estimated at $16.9 million, according to a study by the University of Northern Iowa. RAGBRAI estimates the current economic impact at more than $21 million.

— ◆ —

RAGBRAI is the granddaddy of cross-state bike rides. Many other states have tried to copy it; none has come close. Why did this ride catch on and flourish—and in a state that's not known for setting trends?

RAGBRAI's timing was perfect. A nationwide bicycle boom was cresting around the notion that bikes weren't just for kids anymore. Fourteen million bikes were sold in 1972, fifteen million in 1973 and fourteen million in 1974—more bikes than automobiles in those years. With the nation heading into the Middle East oil crisis, bicycles presented a good way to save money on gas and avoid long lines at filling stations. Also, the first Earth Day was in 1970, and bikes appealed to those concerned about environmental issues. Everyone had to get a new, lightweight ten-speed.

Iowa's vast network of secondary or "farm-to-market" roads is well suited to cycling and covers the state in a comprehensive grid-like pattern.

Iowa towns are numerous and evenly spaced, giving cyclists many opportunities to rest, refresh and revel.

These small towns, many of them struggling to survive, welcome RAGBRAI as a way to make a few bucks and showcase their communities.

Iowa's scenery is varied enough to keep a seven-day ride interesting but uniform enough to allow every part of the state to be included.

Contributing to this statewide experience early on was the *Des Moines Register*, truly "The Newspaper Iowa Depends Upon," as it claimed on its masthead. Its sponsorship of RAGBRAI gave the event instant credibility and extensive exposure across the state.

Also, in terms of timing, the women's movement was in full swing. The National Organization for Women had issued its Bill of Rights in 1968, and both houses of

Congress had passed the Equal Rights Amendment in 1972. Many women discovered new competence and power through RAGBRAI. "What I have enjoyed most on RAGBRAI, especially in the earlier years, was seeing middle-aged women finding independence," Karras wrote later. "RAGBRAI helped demonstrate…that women could pretty much go any damn where they pleased without a guy hanging around." Ironically, Ann Karras, herself, said she went on the first RAGBRAI, in part, because "my husband said I couldn't possibly make that distance."

RAGBRAI's co-founders, John Karras and Donald Kaul, both employed by the *Register*, propelled the ride forward through their coverage. Karras loved road cycling and seemed determined to chronicle RAGBRAI and recognize those who contributed to its success. Donald Kaul got everyone across Iowa talking about RAGBRAI with his witty columns. And the two worked well together. During the first ten years, while

'There must be another big fuel shortage.'

Frank Miller, the *Register*'s cartoonist from 1953 to 1983, drew many cartoons similar to this one with animals commenting on "strange" human behavior during RAGBRAI. Others were captioned: "Every year about this time they all go berserk." "Sometimes it's nice to just be a cow." And "The migratory instinct in people is one of nature's great marvels." *From the* Des Moines Register. *Reprinted with permission.*

Kaul still rode, they would amuse readers by haranguing each other in print about who chose the route, who ordered the weather and who was slacking off.

Here's Kaul on Karras: "Karras's problem is that he speaks for the people who ride at the front of the pack, those who are physically fit and who lead clean, wholesome lives and make lists. I rise to the defense of those in the rear of the pack, a far more insouciant lot." And here's Karras on Kaul: "For me, the day would have been perfect except that Kaul passed me once. True, I was standing still at a lemonade stop, but having Kaul within five miles of wherever I am between 7:00 a.m. and 3:00 p.m. gives me pause. I mean, it's like being passed by Quasimodo." These two riders and writers played their charade to the hilt, and readers loved it.

RAGBRAI was lucky to get off to a good start. Similarly, many RAGBRAIers get off to a good early start each day to avoid the afternoon heat…and to see the sunrise. *Ken Urban Photography.*

Clarence Pickard also helped get RAGBRAI off to a strong start. This unassuming eighty-three-year-old farmer inspired everyone by biking the first year. Overnight, he became a folk hero and had everyone in Iowa following the ride.

RAGBRAI flourished because Iowans are friendly. That may be a cliché, but Iowans' community spirit and open-mindedness make them good hosts. They are kind and generous. Their trusting nature leads them to open their homes to strangers, loan them money and even hand over the car keys! A corollary of this friendliness is that Iowans are courteous drivers, which goes a long way toward encouraging a big bike ride.

Finally, RAGBRAI succeeded because it got lucky. Throwing hundreds, then thousands, of cyclists, most of whom were inexperienced, onto busy highways presented tremendous risks and liabilities. Despite no preparation the first year and minimal planning for the next couple of years, the ride encountered no serious problems early on. In fact, it suffered no fatalities during its first eleven years. If those early years had been marred by crashes, fights, theft, drunkenness or lewd behavior, RAGBRAI would have floundered rather than flourished.

Chapter 1

KARRAS AND KAUL'S CAPER

The First Year

I n 1903, a daily newspaper announced a six-stage bike race. The founders' goal was to sell more newspapers.

In 1973, another daily newspaper announced a six-day bike ride. The founders' goal was to get the newspaper (their employer) to pay for a bicycle jaunt.

Although separated by seven decades and thousands of miles, both these promotions were instant successes—and developed into the two greatest, longest-lasting newspaper promotions ever.

"Anywhere you go in the world, people who know about bikes know two things: the Tour de France and RAGBRAI," says Carter LeBeau, one of the few people who has cycled on all forty RAGBRAIs.

LAUNCHED AS A LARK: THE FIRST YEAR

Some people buy a sports car for their mid-life crisis. John Karras bought a bike.

Married with children, the thirty-seven-year-old Karras purchased a reddish-orange, ten-speed Raleigh Carleton for $125 in 1967. He quickly became fascinated with road biking and later called this fascination a "benign substitute for a mid-life crisis…or perhaps it *was* my mid-life crisis."

In any event, cycling made him feel like a kid, and riding that particular ten-speed was "an epiphany." After turning the pedals once, he coasted and coasted and coasted. "I'm never going to have to pedal this thing," he remembered thinking. "I was hooked."

Karras became a cycling evangelist and soon talked friend and co-worker Donald Kaul into biking. Karras was a night copyeditor at the *Des Moines Register*, and Kaul was a columnist. Like Karras, the middle-aged Kaul took to biking with the zeal of a convert.

Donald Kaul on SAGBRAI in 1974. "If I don't make it, tell Karras I died with his name on my lips—along with a few suggestions," he wrote. *Kaye and Carter LeBeau.*

In one of his popular "Over the Coffee" columns, he described his life *before* cycling: "I got out of bed each morning like a fighter rising at the count of nine. My hand trembled until well into my second cup of coffee, and I tended to black out if I brushed my teeth too vigorously." *After* taking up cycling, it was another story: "Biking has become one of the overriding passions of my life. What Salvation has done for Billy Graham, what Positive Thinking has done for Norman Vincent Peale, what George McGovern did for Richard Nixon, biking has done for me. You, too, can be the envy of all your friends who think golf is a sport. You can even be young again."

In their free time, Karras and Kaul started biking Iowa's backroads. Karras grew up in Cleveland and Kaul in Detroit. What struck the city boys was something that would later strike hundreds of thousands of cyclists on RAGBRAI: the beauty of Iowa's countryside when seen from the seat of a bicycle. "On a bike at ten miles per hour, it was—Wow!" Karras wrote.

During the late 1960s, when bicycling was still considered a childhood activity and long-distance recreational bicycling was virtually unheard of, particularly in the Midwest,

Karras and Kaul were tossing their two-wheelers into (what else?) a Volkswagen bus and exploring Iowa by bike. Karras started calling Iowa a cyclist's paradise.

As they logged more and more miles, their confidence grew. One day in 1971, the intrepid cyclists biked 125 miles from Des Moines to Iowa City. On that tough, thirteen-hour day, the idea of RAGBRAI was born. "Hell, we said, if we can ride to Iowa City in one day, why not cross the whole state in a week?" Karras later recalled.

That's it. There was no lightning bolt or burning bush. Karras and Kaul just thought biking all the way across Iowa would be a fine challenge and a fun escapade. The dynamic duo began plotting ways to do it on company time and have their employer pick up the tab. They first suggested that Kaul participate in some of the fundraising bike rides that were popping up around the state. That idea was never realized. Next, they suggested that they bike together across Iowa and file stories about their experiences. Recognizing the potential for some good publicity and community relations, the *Register* approved the idea for August 1973.

But this was not the first time the paper recognized the bicycle's potential to help sell newspapers and put itself in the center of a story about that two-wheeled contraption. In 1869, a *Register* reporter called for a Des Moines merchant to buy some bicycles, historian John Zeller uncovered. "We want one to run items down with and are willing to pay for it," the reporter wrote. "Des Moines being the fastest city in the State ought to have the first bicycle." Des Moines got its bikes (velocipedes, actually) in 1869, and over the next several years, the *Register* made much of them, publishing many articles about bike races, demonstrations and accidents.

Back to June 1973: the *Register*'s managing editor suggested, almost as an afterthought, that Karras and Kaul invite readers to accompany them as they biked across Iowa. "Good idea," said Karras, not knowing whether it was. Nonetheless, he wrote this invitation, published on July 22, 1973, just one month prior to the ride.

Bike ride across Iowa

Donald Kaul and I are going to ride from Sioux City to Davenport the week of Aug. 26 and we'd like to have as many of you as are able join us along the way. The purpose of the trip, sponsored by our boss, The Des Moines Register, *is to promote cycling on Iowa's great cycling asset, paved secondary roads.*

We're going to ride rain or shine, hot or cold. Each day's ride will leave at 8 a.m. except the hundred-miler to Williamsburg. See you in August.

This low-key invitation generated a surprising amount of interest in what the paper would casually refer to as the Karras-Kaul Bike Ride, the Great Bike Trip, the Great Six-Day Bike Trip and the Great Six-Day Bike Ride Across Iowa. About 250 bicyclists showed up in Sioux City to participate, even if only for a day or two.

The *Des Moines Register* has been covering and promoting bicycles in Iowa since 1869, before high wheels were even invented. *Photo by Scott Russell.*

Alas, the riders discovered that there had been very little planning or preparation. The late Don Benson, who worked in the *Register*'s promotion department, had made hotel reservations for the two leaders. Everyone else was on his or her own—in every way. No provisions had been made for traffic control, medical care, camping, food and drink, bike repairs or transporting gear. The pass-through and overnight towns had not been consulted. And the route had not been traveled in advance; it had just been drawn on a map.

As a result, the ride was fraught with detours and delays, confusion and chaos. Many people simply camped each night on the grounds of the motel where Karras and Kaul stayed. Throughout the week, riders knocked on the leaders' motel room doors complaining of everything from a lost sleeping bag to a lost little brother. Early on, the heat, hills and headwinds were unbearable. Kaul wrote, "You lose salt, you lose water, you lose sugar and finally, you lose your mind."

But somehow it worked. Local residents provided food and drink, often for free. People on and off bikes helped each other. Bill Albright, owner of Bill's Cyclery, came

Clutier, Ia-- 7/24/86 -- Jon Winkelpleck, 16, mows alfalfa on his grandmother's farm Thursday, ignoring RAGBRAI bikers pedaling into a headwind north of here. TAYLOR pic.

Jon Winkelpleck mows alfalfa north of Clutier in 1986. Today, farmers work in air-conditioned tractors equipped with GPS technologies, farms are huge and large confinement lots dot the landscape. *From the* Des Moines Register. *Reprinted with permission.*

on the ride to bike but brought along a van with tires, tubes and tools. At the start and end of each day, he and his team sat outside their hotel repairing bikes.

On day two, the cyclists encountered their first detour. A bridge was out east of Storm Lake, forcing the riders to detour five miles—on gravel. On day three, the riders, including their two leaders, took an ill-advised shortcut along busy U.S. Highway 30 full of fast cars and lumbering trucks.

On day four, about five hundred cyclists biked the easy thirty-eight miles from Ames to Des Moines. The group was so large that the police insisted on escorting it into town but obliged the cyclists to wait until most of them had gathered in one spot. By then, the group was too big to escort through intersections and traffic signals on streets filled with automobilists who were unprepared for a big bunch of bikes. The group became so congested and went so slowly that Kaul fell over, says William Laubengayer. "His foot was stuck in the toe clip and down he went."

Ironically, the day that filled everyone with trepidation was the day things began to click. At a time when hardly anyone had biked a century, day five was 106 miles from Des Moines to Williamsburg. But the terrible heat broke, and the terrain

Carter LeBeau w
his trademark, u
rugby socks, in W
Branch on the *R*
bike ride across
by Carl Voss. From
Moines Register
with permission.

turned out to be gentler than anticipated. Riders survived the long ride, and some even enjoyed the experience.

The ride finished in Davenport, not so much triumphantly but rather with a big sigh of relief. "The mayor was madder than hops because we didn't have the decency to show up when we were 'supposed' to," Laubengayer remembers. At the end, 114 cyclists got in a hastily assembled line to sign up for an official patch that would be mailed to them.

What really sustained these cyclists were the generous helpings of support and encouragement from locals all along the route. They waved, they cheered, they visited. The enthusiastic welcome must have made cyclists feel as though they were cycling an Iowa version of the Tour de France. They concluded that Iowans were incredibly hospitable, even to a band of sweaty strangers on steel steeds.

On that first ride were:

- Carl Voss, a *Register* photographer who was traveling with a mobile darkroom that he had to set up each night in the home where he stayed. Currently, he chairs the Des Moines Bicycle Collective.

- Frank "Huck" Thompson, who went on to become the only person to bike every mile of every RAGBRAI, including the optional loop, for the first thirty-five years. He had been a speed roller skater before taking up cycling, which accounted for his impressive strength and speed. When flu forced him to break his streak, he broke down and wept.

- Bill Wertzberger, eighteen, who lived in Dubuque on Iowa's eastern border, had no other way of getting to the start of the ride in Sioux City, on the western border, so he simply biked there. Then he turned around and biked back to the eastern edge of Iowa with the group. Inadvertently, he inaugurated a tradition of cycling to the starting point that many others have followed to this day.

- Scott Dickson and his brother Randy, both of whom went on to participate in the first forty RAGBRAIs. A champion cyclist, Scott might be America's most compulsive biker. Up until 2008, he cycled every day for twenty-five years.

- LeBeau, who the year before had biked across Wisconsin with friends and liked it so much that he decided to bike across a different state every year. "When I saw the *Register* article [inviting readers to ride with Karras and Kaul], I called my friends and told them we wouldn't have to worry about which state to bike next." After the ride, LeBeau says he "talked it up so much that people thought I had organized it."

FOLK HERO

The most remarkable cyclist on that first ride was eighty-three-year-old Clarence Pickard. The Indianola farmer inspired such epithets as "man of steel," "one hell of a man" and "the George Burns of cycling," the latter due to his age, charm and unadorned wit.

No one would have expected this from the unassuming man who arrived at the start of the ride with a used, girl's ten-speed Schwinn. The bike weighed a heavy 35 pounds, while the five-foot, six-inch Pickard weighed only 116 pounds. Most people wondered if the frail-looking man would make it through the first day. Their doubts increased as the ride began. Pickard rode slowly and fell down often. It came out that he had purchased the bike for this ride and only ridden it "around the block" in preparation. He didn't even know how to shift the gears.

Adding to the doubts was his garb: long trousers; a long-sleeve shirt buttoned to the collar; a long-sleeve sweater *under* the shirt; and a new, five-dollar pair of high-top tennis shoes, which he called "an extravagance." Topping it all off to protect his bald head was a silver pith helmet.

Donald Kaul chats with Clarence Pickard, the eighty-three-year-old retired farmer who biked every mile of the first ride and inspired thousands to follow his example. *From the* Des Moines Register. *Reprinted with permission.*

Pickard said he had decided to join the ride to see Iowa, meet young people and "show that an old person could do something that might surprise other people." He attributed his good health to hard work, a frugal lifestyle and not smoking. His drinks of choice were cold water and milk.

Pickard proved his mettle the first day, riding 72 miles from Sioux City to Storm Lake. He rode slowly but steadily, like the storybook tortoise. His fellow cyclists welcomed him with surprise—and relief. Pickard said he had no doubts about completing the entire ride. When asked about the dreaded 106-mile day from Des Moines to Williamsburg, he simply responded, "I guess I might have to put my lights on before I get there."

After the media praised his steadfastness, the ascetic Pickard gained recognition throughout the state, although he tried to fend off the attention. "I'm not all that phenomenal, as people have been saying," he told Chuck Offenburger, a new reporter at the *Register*. "It's that I've always worked hard—farming, cutting trees, gathering trash—and I'm in good shape."

Pickard's fame increased after he completed the 106-mile ride on Thursday. Actually, he rode more miles than that because he got lost. (It's practically impossible to get lost on RAGBRAI today, but this was understandable the first year because the route was poorly indicated, and there were few other riders indicating the way.) "Heck, we were supposed to go east but I came to a point where Highway 6 turned north," he explained. Pickard ended up on the shoulder of Interstate 80. A state trooper stopped him and helped get him back to the route.

By Friday, the last day of the six-day ride, Pickard was the most talked-about person in Iowa. Locals came out in droves to catch sight of him. Students from Ernest Horn Elementary School in Iowa City lined the road with outstretched hands. When he stopped to acknowledge their cheering, he fell off his bike but quickly stood up, doffed his pith helmet and took a gracious bow.

The young Wertzberger, who had biked across Iowa to start the ride, rode with Pickard part of the last day. "He's really interesting to talk to," Wertzberger said. "He knows a lot about just about everything."

When Pickard finally crossed the finish line in Davenport at about 7:00 p.m., he found more than one hundred well-wishers waiting to witness him complete his 443-mile odyssey. The mayor gave him a Super Senior Citizen of the Day certificate. The still unpretentious Pickard "rolled up the certificate, stuck it in his shirt pocket and proceeded with the business of signing autographs, shaking hands and answering questions," Karras wrote.

"Whatever it was that possessed people, it was genuine and I dogged well better play my role as nicely as I could," Pickard later told the *Register*. "They all wanted to identify with the old man with the silver hat."

Pickard drew a tremendous amount of positive attention to what could have been a throwaway story about a ragtag group of "crazies" biking across Iowa. And he did it with panache. More importantly, he encouraged others to test their limits. As Kaul put it in one of his widely read columns, "By the end of the day, everyone's tired and hates each other. But the one thing that keeps you going is that long after you've quit riding, somewhere back there—and still riding—is Mr. Pickard, and he's smiling. He's 83 years old, and if he can make it, then, by God, the rest of us can, too."

MODERN-DAY CLARENCE

Clarence Boesenberg wears a bike helmet rather than a pith helmet, but he shares many traits with the legendary Clarence Pickard. Boesenberg rode his first full RAGBRAI

Clarence Boesenberg, a modern-day Clarence Pickard, rode his first full RAGBRAI in 2012 at the age of eighty-six. He wore this jersey supporting World Bicycle Relief every day. *Ken Urban Photography.*

in 2012 at the age of eighty-six. He had ridden one day a couple of times before but would never leave his wife's side for more than a day at a time. She had a stroke twenty-nine years previously, and Boesenberg says he "had the privilege of taking care of her" until she died in 2011.

After waiting so long for the opportunity to ride RAGBRAI, Boesenberg wanted to make sure he would succeed. To prepare, the 145-pound, five-foot-ten-inch Boesenberg trained some 3,600 miles, including a few 100-mile rides and some hot days. He did well on RAGBRAI XL, despite the extreme heat and the fact that he was riding on knees that were replaced in 2007 and on his grandson's ten-speed Schwinn that was built in 1979. "Everyone in my family says I should have a fancy new bike, but I get along fine on this one," Boesenberg says. "It's better than the one I had before that I bought at a garage sale for five dollars."

Different family members biked with Boesenberg each day of the ride, and they camped along the way, except the night RAGBRAI overnighted in his hometown of Cedar Rapids. "I was sure glad to sleep in my own bed that night," Boesenberg says.

One day he ran across another elderly rider and said to him, "You're pretty old to be doing this." That rider happened to be eighty-six-year-old LeBeau. "We had a good laugh when we found out that he was a bit younger than me," Boesenberg says.

Boesenberg plans to ride RAGBRAI as long as possible. That could be for many years considering that his mother rode a three-wheel bike until she died at the age of ninety-nine.

Chapter 2

STILL CRAZY AFTER FORTY YEARS

RAGBRAI's Best Stories

Everyone who's done RAGBRAI has stories, so let's continue with some of the best stories about this world-class county fair on wheels. When I started collecting RAGBRAI stories, I wrote down every one about a wallet full of cash that was returned intact, a rider who happened to meet an old acquaintance and locals who opened their homes to strangers, even when they were not home. I was soon overwhelmed because such stories are legion. The following stories are a cut above the rest. They reveal RAGBRAI's rich spirit and will set the stage for the rest of the history.

* On the penultimate day of the 464-mile RAGBRAI III, a dirty, distressed young woman approached co-founder John Karras. It was very hot, and she was sunburned, despite being slathered with suntan lotion. She hobbled toward Karras, limping, with one shoulder lower than the other, as he recounted in *RAGBRAI: Everyone Pronounces It Wrong*, by John and Ann Karras.

  Thinking to himself, "My God, this woman should be in the hospital," Karras got up to offer her his seat.

  "Are you John Karras?" she asked.

  "Yes," Karras answered, with some trepidation.

  "I just want you to know what a great time I'm having," she said. "I hope you do this again next year."

* On RAGBRAI III, Steve Kobberdahl's dad improvised a clever way of getting the family's car to the end of the route. Each night he drove the car ahead to the next overnight town and hitchhiked back to the family's campsite. He carried the front wheel of his bike as a prop to get cars to stop. "Everyone assumed he had a bike problem, and he always got a ride right away," Steve said.

* In 1974, Chuck Dick was running for U.S. representative from Iowa's Fourth District. Perhaps one reason he later lost to Neal Smith was that his campaign signs along the road were less effective than they should have been. His signs

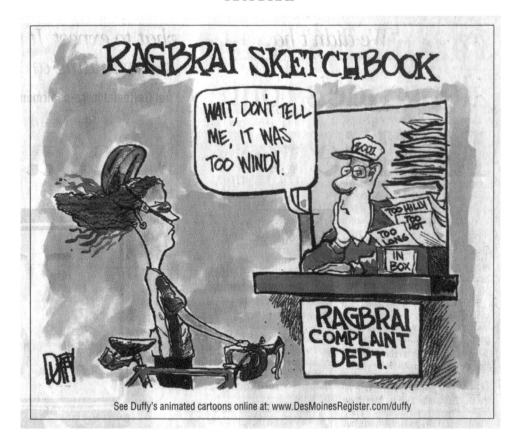

Complaining is not encouraged on RAGBRAI. "If you're not having a good time, lower your standards," says Brad Prendergast, C.U.B.S. leader. *From the* Des Moines Register. *Reprinted with permission.*

simply said "Chuck Dick," which many RAGBRAI riders thought was a reference to President Richard Nixon, then near the end of his Watergate travail.

- On the first day in 1979, a storm drenched RAGBRAI cyclists. After it stopped, a muddy, grimy group of thirty riders stopped in Hartley to wash their clothes. But they couldn't very well strip at the coin laundry. To the rescue was local resident David Skattebo, who had just finished several loads of laundry. He handed out his freshly cleaned clothes so all the riders could take off and wash their dirty clothes. After they left, Skattebo did his laundry, again.

- On RAGBRAI III, eighteen-year-old Penn Whitlow's bike broke down. While he and his friend were looking over the bike, Grace Montgomery drove up and offered them a lift to the bike shop, co-founder Donald Kaul recounted in the *Register*. Montgomery had a meeting to attend, so she stopped there and told the boys to drive themselves to the shop. "Don't you even want to know our names?" one of the boys asked. She didn't.

Alas, the shop was closed, but the boys were able to contact the owner, who called an employee and asked him to go in and repair the bike. The cost was only eight dollars, about the cost of the part. They drove to Montgomery's meeting place and waited for her to finish. She then drove them several miles farther along the route—but not before asking them whether they needed any money.

"You don't see much of that sort of thing going on in New York City, or any place else for that matter," Kaul concluded.

- Bob Frey was known as a funny guy, but this time the joke was on him. He was heavy, a "belly bumper," as his friend Carter LeBeau described him. One year, Frey purchased an eighteen-pound titanium bicycle, one of the first such ultra-lightweight bikes to appear on RAGBRAI. Every evening, his teammates surreptitiously poured a handful of lead shot into the seat tube. "The bike must have weighed thirty pounds before Frey finally understood why he was having so much trouble on the hills," LeBeau said.

- One year, leaving the starting town, two riders from New York City approached Don Benson, the RAGBRAI coordinator, recounts Jim Green, his successor. They asked what to do if they had to pee and there were no bathrooms or kybos at hand. "Just go in the cornfield," Benson said. Shortly afterward, Benson saw one of the men, clearly visible, peeing in a soybean field.

Iowans have a corny sense of humor.

RAGBRAI

- Near Grafton on RAGBRAI XV, sheriff's deputies were flagging down cyclists. About a mile away, eighteen-month-old Amanda Alitz had chased a kitten into a huge cornfield, and the toddler was missing for three hours. The officers were asking for help, and the response was immediate, observers told the *Register*. At least 250 RAGBRAIers biked to the farm and lined up along the edge of the 180-acre cornfield. On orders, the riders walked in unison toward the other end of the field, half a mile away, calling Amanda's name.

     As they neared the end, a motorist spotted the little girl exiting the field. He picked her up and took her home. "When the girl heard all those people coming toward her, she probably got scared and started moving away from us," said Leo Dorsey, one of the officers. "As hot as it was out there, she would not have lasted much longer."

- "When you organize to host a RAGBRAI visit, there's some fear and mistrust that you have to deal with," said Harris Honsey, co-chair in the small Norwegian community of Lake Mills, when RAGBRAI passed through in 2005. "People say, 'What? You're bringing 12,000 people to town? How are you going to get enough lutefisk for that many people?' But I reminded them that the good thing about lutefisk is you can't tell if it's spoiled."

- One day, Brian Duffy, the *Register*'s cartoonist and RAGBRAI co-host, was riding behind a young man who wore nothing but a loincloth and shoes. "As we passed a retirement home, he was waving at a group of little old ladies who were smiling and waving back," Duffy said. "But as they realized what he was wearing, their hands dropped at the same time as their jaws dropped."

- Mike Clousing wore a video camera on his helmet to share RAGBRAI with family and friends, and Shelly Longhorn, his fiancée, edited the tapes. That seemed like a good idea except Mike often forgot that he had the camera on his helmet and the recording device in the back pocket of his jersey. He inadvertently recorded himself singing, visiting the kybo and panting up hills, with low cadence and heart rate monitors ringing in the background. And Shelly caught Mike looking at the same girl for twenty minutes. "O.K. She was cute, but not twenty-minutes cute," she told him.

- Tai Blas, who has been blind since birth, does RAGBRAI because she "likes to do things that people wouldn't expect a blind person to do, like downhill skiing and rock climbing." Rather than dwelling on the negative, she talks about the positive side of being "disabled." For example, on RAGBRAI she can tweet and blog using a small keyboard *while riding* on the back of her tandem, which is piloted by a volunteer from Adaptive Sports Iowa. "No one else biking RAGBRAI can do that," she said.

     When asked if she had any complaints at all about RAGBRAI, she answered jokingly, "Sure, listening to the able-bodied people complaining about things."

- When Kaye and Carter LeBeau married in 1995, she was not much of a cyclist, but he had already done twenty-two RAGBRAIs. "I put it in our prenup that she had to become a cyclist," Carter joked.

- Participants were surprised in 1982 to see a monkey riding on the handlebars of David Taylor's bike. Taylor was socializing Pepper, the monkey, getting him used to being around a lot of people as preparation for Helping Hands, a program that trains monkeys to help quadriplegics. "Monkeys can do a lot for the disabled: turn on lights, feed them and fetch things," Taylor explained. A few years later, Pepper was, indeed, accepted into the Helping Hands training program.

- On his first RAGBRAI, Rich Ketcham had some saddle sores. One day, after finishing the optional century loop, he was sitting in a city park sprinkling a little talcum powder into his shorts when the lid fell off and the whole bottle emptied into his shorts. "Walking around after that, I looked like Pigpen [a Peanuts character who always left behind clouds of dirt]," he said.

- On RAGBRAI XII, Dick Schuler had run out of cash and did not have a credit card with him. He walked into a bank—a bank, mind you—and walked out a few minutes later with $100. No, he didn't use a gun to secure the money—just a promise to repay it, *Register* reporter Chuck Offenburger wrote. Schuler also had to promise not to reveal the name of the bank, which was concerned about setting a precedent.

- When Lance Armstrong rode RAGBRAI for the first time in 2006, he spoke in Newton to a crowd of twenty thousand, one of RAGBRAI's largest crowds. "So this is RAGBRAI," he was reported to have told the crowd. "Why did I waste my last seven years in France?" If only he had realized that sooner!

- In 2004, Oliver Borzo (the author's nephew) biked into Marshalltown, well ahead of his group. He found the street where he and his group were supposed to spend the night, and he found the house with their van parked in front. He knocked on the door, but nobody was home. Since the door was unlocked, Oliver went in, made himself at home and took a shower. When he was drying off, with only a towel wrapped around his midsection, the owner walked in and asked Oliver, "What are you doing in my house?" That's right; Oliver was in the wrong house. With RAGBRAI in full swing, they parted amicably. Oliver went off (fully clothed) and found the right house.

- In 1993, George Day rode a recumbent with his dog Smooch perched on the back. Whenever Day hit a steep hill, he would snap his fingers, and the forty-seven-pound dog, attached with a long leash, would hop off and help pull the bike.

- In 1983, RAGBRAI veteran Al Culbert was surprised one morning to find a young blond woman sleeping next to him in his tent when he woke up. The night before, she had wandered into the wrong tent. Culbert had heard someone come in but thought it was his son, who usually turned in much later than he did. (Culbert never did find out where his son spent that night.)

Over the years, riders have trained more and more for RAGBRAI…and ridden increasingly sophisticated bikes. *Photo by Bob Frank.*

- RAGBRAI has passed through more than 780 communities in Iowa. On its fortieth anniversary, RAGBRAI finally got around to passing through Lohrville (population 368). For its theme, the town chose: "Welcome to Lohrville, The Ride's 40-Year-Old Virgin."
- In 2012, temperatures on RAGBRAI hit 106, in the shade—but without any shade along the road! The Weather Channel offered tips for coping with the extreme heat: stay indoors, don't exercise, avoid alcohol and drink lots of water. Guess which three tips everyone ignored.
- Some teams take their training seriously. Team Me Off was known for its "century" training ride every March. They held it in a bar and used a stationary bike to reach one hundred miles—as a team, not individually. Members took turns moving from barstool to bike seat.
- Kenneth Smith used to blame his poor memory for doing RAGBRAI. At the end of each ride, he swore he'd never go through it again. But by the following spring he would always forget how tough it was and sign up again. In the end, Smith could be excused for his poor memory. He was eighty-four years old when he rode his thirty-second RAGBRAI.
- In 2005, Saul Hammond strong-armed his way across Iowa. An automobile crash had damaged his spinal cord, so he rode a hand cycle. "End of the first day, I'm

thinking my arms might fall off," he said. "End of the second day, I'm hoping they do because they hurt so much."

- Every year, RAGBRAI shares its profits with the overnight communities. In 1996, Sibley used $4,500 of its $7,500 check to buy every elementary school student in Sibley and nearby Ocheyedan, all 650 of them, a bike helmet. Additional funds for helmets came from criminal fines levied on three out-of-state cyclists convicted of possession of marijuana and theft during the ride.

- One of the more exceptional cyclists on RAGBRAI XIII was twenty-year-old Jeff Henderson. This ride took him to his fifteenth state on a tour he was making of all fifty states. In addition to carrying his camping gear and a guitar, he lugged window-washing equipment to earn money along the way.

- Rhonda Pedley found her family through RAGBRAI. Born in Iowa City and adopted in Dubuque, Pedley figured that her biological mother might be from northeastern Iowa. All she knew was her mother's name, which is unusual. When she noticed that RAGBRAI XIII was going to pass through northeastern Iowa, she asked her boyfriend to check phone books along the route for anyone with that name. He found one such person in Manchester, who ultimately led Pedley to her biological mother and a reunion with the rest of her newfound kin.

- In 1995, for the fourth RAGBRAI in a row, the Jacobsen family of seven slept each night in their livestock trailer, which usually carried hogs to market. "We clean it up real well," said Dean Jacobsen, who installed bunk beds, a rollout canopy, a foldout table and carpeting for his family. "You know you're in the right state when you come for RAGBRAI and see a farm family sleeping in their stock trailer."

- One morning on RAGBRAI, a storm blew in as the Pork Belly Ventures charter was breaking camp. The strong wind billowed tents, and a few tents that had been unstaked lifted up and blew away. "One fellow chasing his tent sees me and says, 'I love RAGBRAI!'" recounted Pete Phillips, PBV's founder.

- Shanda South had seen RAGBRAI for years but only through the window of a car. She wanted to do RAGBRAI, but at 300 pounds, she didn't feel comfortable on a bike. Finally, at the age of thirty-four, she decided to do the ride and started dieting and training. Within a year, she had lost 140 pounds. "I pretty much lost a whole person to do this," she said as she biked RAGBRAI XXVIII.

- RAGBRAI is infectious. Wendy Lee happened to be visiting her stepmother in Mount Pleasant in 2009 when the ride rolled into town. She noticed massage tables being set up and said to herself, "If there's a massage at the end of each day, maybe I could do this." Later, while still trying to talk herself into doing the ride, she said to a friend, "I think I'll do it in five years."

  "Honey, you could be dead in five years. Do it this year." And she did.

- Steve Stevens rode his 1886 high wheel across the state in 1994. With a fifty-four-inch-diameter front wheel, the bike is just one in his collection of twenty high wheels. One day, he broke the bike's left handle pulling up a hill. A girl on the side of the road said, "My dad can fix that." He did, welding the handle back on for no charge, and the big wheel kept on turning.

- One of the zaniest activities on RAGBRAI was a toilet bowl race in 2001. Toilets were mounted on three-wheel dollies, and contestants propelled themselves with ski poles that had toilet plungers at the end. When one contestant wobbled off course, the judge barked, "I hope you ride a bicycle better than that." When a man in an Elvis costume won, the judge proclaimed, "Every King deserves his throne."

- One year Carter LeBeau and some friends took a detour, staying overnight in a town off the route. The next morning, while retracing their path to catch up with RAGBRAI, they biked through a town that RAGBRAI had passed through the day before. When they stopped for breakfast, they heard a local resident say with a grimace, "Oh, my. They're coming back!"

- In 1998, the Boone Speedway was not the official RAGBRAI campsite, but that didn't stop promotions director Jeff Lawton from posting signs trying to lure in teams and charters. The signs offered free beer to drivers who brought campers in with them, but Lawton said his offer didn't amount to bribery. "I'd call it direct marketing," he told the *Register*.

- Wayne Vader rode his bike off the road just one mile short of Clinton, the final destination of RAGBRAI VI. After biking 439 miles, he had to ride the last mile in an ambulance.

- Tom Kurth managed to lose his tent in his own backyard. His Iowa Valley Bicycle Club teammates like to hide his tent every night, putting it on goalposts, the top of other team buses, etc. Kurth goes along with the prank and often wears a T-shirt that says, "I'm Tom. Can you help me find my tent?" In 2012, he hosted the C.U.B.S. in his backyard in Marshalltown. That was the first time he had hosted a team, so he did a lot of socializing, got distracted and failed to stake down his tent adequately. A storm kicked up and blew his tent away. Or did someone move it? Luckily, he was able to sleep in his house that night. The next morning, he found his tent in a field.

- Carl Voss, who was on the first RAGBRAI, cycled into Jefferson in 1989 and saw a teenage girl selling homemade vanilla ice cream with a kick of lemon. She told him she was raising money to pay off the insurance deductible from an automobile accident. She also hoped to raise extra money to buy some clothes before heading off to college in a couple of weeks.

    "I felt I should help her," Voss says, "so I had eight dishes, a dollar each, one after another. I guess I was there a while."

- RAGBRAI attracts all kinds, even thieves. In 1991, the ride passed through Pella, which gave sixty-eight-year-old M.L. "Moppy" Dudek the opportunity to return a sign he had stolen fifty-one years earlier. "I guess I've felt a little guilty ever since,"

Feeding twenty thousand hungry cyclists is always a challenge for a small town. *From the* Des Moines Register. *Reprinted with permission.*

Dudek told the *Register*. Mayor Johnny Menninga graciously accepted the two-foot-long yellow sign shaped like a wooden shoe that said, "Pella 3 miles."

• In Dike during RAGBRAI XXXVIII, cyclists Tim Lane, Jim Hart and Steve Quirk were taking a break when a local woman pulled her Ford pickup off the road with a flat tire. She had no jack or spare, so the three cyclists found several large pieces of wood and hoisted a corner of the pickup onto some cinder blocks. They sent the woman and her passenger into town to get the flat fixed. "That was easy…we may as well rotate the tires," one of them joked. But that's what they did! "In every state of the union, someone will eventually help you fix your flat tire, but only in Iowa will we rotate your tires," Lane said.

Chapter 3

WHAT IT'S ALL ABOUT

An Overview

The second "R" in RAGBRAI stands for ride, not race. While many participants rush through the day's allotted miles, most follow a leisurely pace. The first time John Becker did RAGBRAI in 2002, he got up early, rode fast and didn't stop until reaching the next overnight town. "Some of the pass-through towns weren't even set up," he says. But in 2007, when he rode it for the first time with his wife, Sue, they stopped everywhere, took pictures and participated in activities. "It was much more enjoyable," he says. "We loved the Mayberry feeling, the Fourth of July every day."

Despite an average length of 472 miles, RAGBRAI is within most people's ability because each day is broken up by opportunities to stop. Some riders stop to "smell the roses," others to smell the "Buds." In fact, it's hard *not* to stop for activities such as tossing a skillet in Macksburg, home of the annual National Skillet Throw Festival, or placing a bet on where a chicken will defecate in a rousing round of chicken poop bingo.

The roads along each year's route are well-maintained, two-lane state and county highways. They're not closed to traffic, but most locals choose other roads the day RAGBRAI rolls through. The extremely supportive Iowa State Patrol watches over the ride and helps cyclists cross busy highway intersections.

THE RIDERS AND THEIR BIKES

For the sake of safety and in consideration of the small size of most Iowa towns, RAGBRAI caps the number of riders at 10,000 per day, selling 8,500 weeklong passes and 1,500 day passes per day. Occasionally, the road fills up with bikes, but usually the ribbon of riders stretches over many miles, dispersing the cyclists.

In 2012, Drew Buck rode a bike geared so he had to pedal backward to go uphill. The fifty-pound bike was made in the 1920s by St Etienne in France. The onions on Buck's handlebars are in recognition of "Onion Johnnies," French laborers who used to sell onions door-to-door in Great Britain. "Everyone encourages you, and that's worth a lot of drugs," Buck says of his experiences riding the bike. *Photo by Scott Russell.*

RAGBRAI riders range in age from infants (carried in a seat or pulled in a wagon) to octogenarians. At least one nonagenarian has ridden, ninety-year-old Walter Dutton, who rode in 1996 with his granddaughter. The average age of participants has been ticking up but may have plateaued at about forty-five since the early 2000s.

RAGBRAI cyclists are extremely varied: fit or fat; total lush or teetotaler; young prankster or old codger. Some jump on the ride for one day while others make RAGBRAI part of a cross-country sojourn.

Some participants are serious cyclists who train hard, while others blow the cobwebs off a borrowed bike and hit the pavement. One rider boasted that her training consisted of mowing the lawn, but training is no guarantee of success. Joshua Schamberger had eight RAGBRAIs under his belt and in 2012 had ridden two thousand miles training for XL. Nonetheless, he ended up in the hospital due to dehydration.

RAGBRAI is the ultimate BYOB(ike). In the early years, most people rode whatever was lying around their garages or basements. Forrest Ridgway, a bike mechanic on the second ride, remembers that many repairs were required just to make bicycles functional during the first few days. "Neither bikes nor bikers were prepared for the ride," he says. Subsequently, riders started showing up on better bikes, in particular, new ten-speeds.

Today, the bikes come in all shapes and sizes, and some cost several thousands of dollars. Most common are modern road bikes with, say, eighteen to twenty-seven gears and smooth, easy shifting. There are still a lot of old ten-speeds but only a few clunkers, three-speeds and folding bikes. Kathy Schubert likes her folder, primarily because it keeps her schnauzer, Suzy, close to the ground. Recumbents are increasingly popular as baby boomers age. Trikes and tandems always make a good showing, and there have been more hand cycles in recent years.

Beyond that, the RAGBRAI bikes can be amazing, such as a recumbent with a full awning and a trike rigged with a large sail. In 2001, Jack Gannett rode a close-to-the-ground recumbent trike with an aerodynamic shell. "People are suspicious," he said. "They keep asking if I have an engine in here."

John Campbell, sports director with KCRG-TV in Cedar Rapids, rode "Old Yeller," what might be the most famous bicycle in Iowa. He bought the yellow ten-speed at Sears in

Kathy Schubert's schnauzer, Suzy, was on her fourth RAGBRAI in 2012. She's a great icebreaker and poses here with cameraman Rob Rhodes from KCTV in Fairway, Kansas, riding with the Tall Dog Bike Club. *Photo by Kathy Schubert.*

1970 and hardly ever used it until 1994, when his station assigned him to cover RAGBRAI. "I dug it out of the basement and covered the whole ride from that old bike for fourteen years," he says. When Campbell retired in 2012, the station gave him a new bike. "Now I have to decide whether to be loyal to Old Yeller or go off with the new gal," he jokes.

Another famous bicycle on RAGBRAI also happens to be yellow. The recumbent trike looks like a banana and is ridden by Mike Knox, the famous "Banana Man." He started riding RAGBRAI in 1999. One day in 2005, he donned a banana costume he had found in a closet at Kum & Go where he worked. "It made people laugh, and that made the ride easier so I stuck with the theme," Knox says.

In 2009, he added to the costume by putting a banana skin around his recumbent trike. Since then, he's outfitted a fleet of banana bikes, including a tandem trike. Also, he's acquired many more banana costumes, so he often appears with a "bunch" of friends and family in costume. They've pulled plenty of stunts, such as running races, squeezing nine bananas into a kybo and running around in a cornfield where RAGBRAIers can see the tops of their costumes bouncing around. Knox once handed

"Banana Man" Mike Knox has been entertaining RAGBRAI since 2005. Today he has a fleet of bananacyles and travels with "bunches" of friends and family dressed as bananas. *Photo by Scott Russell.*

out bananas donated by HyVee, a grocery-store chain, but told people he couldn't eat one because that would be "bannibalism."

The banana trikes are quite heavy, so Knox travels slowly, so slow that sometimes he has to start his day at 3:00 a.m. to get all the miles in. His slow pace can inspire other riders. One year, a paraplegic riding a hand cycle told Banana Man, "You made my day. When I saw your little flag up ahead I knew I'd pass at least one person today."

Also remarkable is the occasional rider on a trendy fixed-gear bike or an old-fashioned high wheel, both of which require you to keep your feet on the pedals, even downhill (unless you put your feet on the handlebars). It's equally hard to negotiate RAGBRAI's hills and crowds on a tall bike, a jerry-rigged bicycle made of two or more frames welded together with the rider perched high atop, but that doesn't stop cyclists from trying every year.

A few riders have been spotted carrying large blow-up dolls, from an inflatable hag to Barbie to sex toys. In 2000, Jeff Miller rode a tandem with doll Wilimena Rubberta, "for the fun of it." And in 2009, Jordan Rayboy rode with a blow-up doll that he "fondly" named after his real-life wife, Jeska.

At least a blow-up doll is not as heavy as a canoe, such as the thirty-eight-pound, seventeen-foot-long one Mark Dunagan pulled in 2000. Saying that it wasn't just a way to meet girls, he admitted it was a "conversation starter." And Dean "Bareback" Mathias, sixty-one, rides a bike with no seat. "I've always been a runner and that carried over to the cycling," he told the *Quad Cities Dispatch/Argus*. "I usually rode in a high gear, standing up a lot, so this worked out."

Perhaps more difficult than riding RAGBRAI on a high wheel or tall bike is tackling the miles and hills on a skateboard, elliptical bicycle or roller blades or by running. Nevertheless, many people do so. At least they don't end up with a sore butt from sitting. What's next, a pogo stick?

Devin skateboarded RAGBRAI XL to raise money so his brother could go to Special Olympics. From high wheels to tall bikes, single-speeds to thirty-speeds, unicycles to antiques, and roller blades to skateboards, RAGBRAI has seen it all.

RAGBRAI

The Towns and Their Residents

From Ackley to Zingle, Iowa towns have thrown open their arms and doors to RAGBRAI. Some barely existed, and others would not exist for much longer after RAGBRAI's visit (but never because of RAGBRAI's visit!).

Most host towns go all out to clean up their streets and spiff up their buildings in preparation. In 1997, Milton (population 506) demolished six deserted buildings and planted grass and flowers in their place. It instituted volunteer cleaning days, hauled away debris and put students to work painting, raking and mowing. "The spirit here now is better than it's been in years," said Mayor Mike Harrelson. RAGBRAI co-host Chuck Offenburger organized a RAGBRAI volunteer weekend that brought a large crew of workers to Milton from all over Iowa to clean, paint and plant.

Towns decorate to welcome RAGBRAI and make them stand out. In Cedar Rapids in 1990, more than sixty volunteers threw themselves into making a six-story-tall cyclist out of fourteen thousand balloons and hundreds of feet of cable. In addition, towns welcome riders with generous treats. In 1996, Charles City, home of Sara Lee and "Chuck Town" for the day (in honor of Chuck Offenburger), gave away ten thousand pieces of apple pie.

Clever themes set a celebratory tone. In 1993, Manchester's theme was "Crossing the Delaware," in this case Delaware County, of which Manchester is the seat. The mayor greeted riders dressed as George Washington. In Beaman, it was "You're Not Dreamin'. You're in Beaman." One year, Hartley came up with the bike-specific theme of "Get Pumped in Hartley."

Also, towns are smart to highlight their local assets, such as a famous resident, cultural heritage or remarkable building. The five times RAGBRAI concluded in Burlington, the town featured Snake Alley, once recognized as the world's most crooked street. Most of those years, riders were allowed to bike down the steep, switch-backed, brick street, but I prefer riding up, as RAGBRAI did in 2009. (The street was built in 1894 to connect downtown with a neighborhood located up a steep hill during an era when many other cities around the country, including Sioux City, Iowa, were building cable car lines to accomplish the same thing.)

It takes a tremendous effort to host RAGBRAI and even more to pull off elaborate preparations. Many local residents put in an amazing number of hours during the six months leading up to the invasion, and most of those hours are volunteered. In 1998, the overnight town of Boone recruited five hundred volunteers and was still looking for more at the last minute. More than two hundred people volunteered in Storm Lake when RAGBRAI overnighted there in 2001, and some of them put in twenty-five hours a week from February through July.

To prepare residents for the coming horde, towns hold meetings, post notices and go door-to-door along the route. One strategy is to engage as many locals as possible

Biking *up* Burlington's steep, twisty Snake Alley was a fitting finish for RAGBRAI XXXVII. *Ken Urban Photography.*

as volunteers, J.D. Mullen, director of Ankeny's Chamber of Commerce, told the *Register* in 2000. "We thought if they were involved they probably wouldn't complain."

Not all towns and businesses are enamored of RAGBRAI, which can turn a town inside out. Residents fear traffic jams, loud music and rowdy crowds. In 1991, a Marengo resident wrote to the *Register*, "No one felt safe until the bike riders were gone." Another complained of "riders drinking beer from paper cups and cans on the streets, and throwing the empties on the street…and a girl riding down the street without a top on her body."

To minimize the anxiety and inconvenience, some families leave town or hibernate during the twelve- or twenty-four-hour incursion. "It took me twenty-five minutes to cross town, and it usually takes five," said Tammy Hansard, when RAGBRAI came through Ottumwa in 2000. "I'm going to stay out of this mess and watch *ER* tonight."

Some stores, restaurants and even taverns don't want to deal with the crowds and use "sign language" to communicate that sentiment by hanging "Closed" on the door of their business. In 2000, Shorty's Dog Pound, a tavern on Pella's town square, and Benchwarmers, a popular Ankeny tavern, sat out RAGBRAI. In 1997, Joan Tuttle closed her popular café in Millerton the day RAGBRAI came through town. "They came through here sixteen years ago, and a lot of them didn't pay for their food," she said.

Whole towns can lose on RAGBRAI, too. To prepare for the deluge, a town has to go out on a limb investing in law enforcement, sanitation, insurance, a beverage garden, entertainment and T-shirts hoping to make a profit—but without any guarantee they will even recoup their investment, which typically exceeds $100,000 for an overnight town. "Towns should be prudent," said Dan Offenburger, vice-president of the Shenandoah Chamber and Industry Association in 2003. "We've heard of towns losing their shirts because of unrealistic expectations."

A well-run program tends to make money, however. The four times Coralville hosted RAGBRAI, it made between $30,000 and $60,000. "People here get it," says Joshua Schamberger, president of the Iowa City/Coralville Area Convention and Visitors Bureau.

Usually, restaurants, bars, churches and community organizations make more money from RAGBRAI than do the towns, especially when the organizers favor local businesses. In 1997, Indianola issued permits for selling food and merchandise during RAGBRAI only to residents and businesses located in Warren County.

Still, Robert Sack, chair of Manchester's RAGBRAI committee in 1999, says the benefits of RAGBRAI go far beyond the profits a community earns in one day. "RAGBRAI is one of the most exciting programs for economic development that the state of Iowa has ever come up with."

The greatest rewards from hosting RAGBRAI, however, are typically a town's increased community spirit, improved organizational skills and new sense of confidence to tackle other projects. In that sense, RAGBRAI is a success for a town—even before a single cyclist appears on the horizon.

The Entertainment and Activities

The sights and sounds, fun and games along the way can be extremely entertaining. Some of the activities are predictable, such as karaoke and the Hokey Pokey. Some are repeated over the years, such as Elvis impersonators and yellow brick roads. Some are de rigueur, such as a visit to President Herbert Hoover's birthplace in West Branch or the Grotto of the Redemption in West Bend. And some take a page out of Middle America, such as a barn raising or an auction of homemade quilts.

The most memorable entertainment involves one-off creative stunts, such as the seven-block-long cake in 1990 in Algona and the snow volleyball in 2000 in Ankeny, with its "Christmas in July" theme. Ginny Procuniar is not the only one who remembers the square-dancing tractors during RAGBRAI XXIX. Eight old Farmall tractors from Nemaha do-si-do'ed in the middle of a large intersection in Atlantic. Eight men, half dressed as women, drove the tractors, and each couple

With a proud Dutch heritage, Orange City put on a mini version of its May Tulip Festival for
RAGBRAI XL.

wore matching colors. "It was iconic Iowa," Procuniar says. So was a tractor-pull
with a twist: the tractors were the small kind with pedals. Although cyclists didn't
need any more pedaling, plenty of them volunteered to participate.

Singing groups of fake nuns also draw crowds. Years ago, there were the Merry
Sisters from St. Athanasius Church in Jesup, singing old favorites. "We do this as a
tribute to the nuns who taught us in school," said Pat Weber, aka Sister Merry Music.
"They were good, charitable women." In the mid-1990s, there were the Singing Nuns
as well as the Sisters of the Ding-a-Ling, twelve dancing and lip-synching performers.
And let's not forget Nuns on the Run.

On the serious side, many riders visit churches in host communities. Churches not
only prepare food but also schedule services and go out of their way to welcome riders.
"Helping during RAGBRAI is part of our mission…administering to and reaching
out to these people," says Kate Schlenger, a member of Grace United Methodist
Church in Marcus who has ridden five RAGBRAIs herself.

An extremely popular booth along the route every day since 2002 is run by the Iowa
Conservation Team offering free postcards and postage so riders can jot a note to
loved ones the old-fashioned way. Some riders address one of these colorful postcards
celebrating the environment and Iowa's bountiful natural resources to themselves as
a souvenir.

Rather disconcerting, booths in Redfield and Dallas Center in 2000 were signing up organ donors. Equally puzzling was a booth in Shenandoah in 2003 that must have appeared odd for anyone who had biked fifty-seven miles from Glenwood or planned to bike sixty-five miles to Bedford the next day: a Red Cross blood drive.

The Food

Riders who donated blood that day in Shenandoah would have found plenty to rebuild their strength on this all-Iowa picnic on wheels. RAGBRAI's smorgasbord is a bigger draw than the bicycling for some participants who view the biking as just a convenient way to get from one food stand to another.

This bikers' banquet is so copious that many people gain weight on the ride. It's said that only on RAGBRAI could you bike five hundred miles and end up with a new "spare tire." Most riders follow Carl Voss's RAGBRAI See Food Diet: "See food, eat it." And why not? Burning five thousand calories a day, they figure (sometimes incorrectly) that they can eat anything they want.

On RAGBRAI, food always seems to be within arm's reach.

The cornucopia includes pancakes and smoothies, hot dogs, hamburgers and homemade ice cream. More exotic are the breakfast burrito; Maid-Rite (an Iowa-style sloppy joe); and "walking taco," a bag of tortilla chips cut down the middle and loaded with various taco fillings.

Not all the pies are homemade, but it's worth the hunt to find those that are. Voss, official pie judge from 1998 to 2003, sampled up to seventeen slices per day. He found a fabulous pie on RAGBRAI XXXI in Melcher and tracked down the recipe. "It went like this," Voss says: "Butcher hog. Render lard. Pick fruit from your orchard…Now that's really home baking!"

After cycling, a body needs to replenish calcium, potassium and sodium, and eating a baked potato loaded with bacon, cheese and sour cream is a tastier way to achieve this than chugging sports drinks. But don't go looking for butter. Instead, you'll find margarine, which is made of corn oil. Iowa is not primarily a dairy state.

The large variety of ethnic food is a testament to Iowa's rich ethnic heritage. Participants enjoy Dutch letters (almond pastries), Danish kringla, Polish kolaches, German bratwurst and other cultural treats.

Churches, scout troops, fraternal organizations, clubs, schools and community groups prepare and serve much of RAGBRAI's feast, raising precious funds for

Firefighters in Oxford Junction serve up ravenous riders during RAGBRAI XL.

projects and facilities. Recently, health regulations have hampered their ability to participate as freely as in the past.

For-profit vendors, most of them local, also get into the act. The largest ones travel with RAGBRAI, setting up gauntlets of food each day. Riders often start the day with hotcakes from Chris Cakes or Pancake Man. Both use a large griddle with a gantry-style batter dispenser capable of dropping four dollops of batter at a time, thereby making a couple thousand pancakes an hour. Their chefs are known to toss pancakes onto their customers' plates from afar.

Pasta Pastafari serves up pasta with loud reggae music. The unlikely pairing is due to the fact that Italy once dominated Ethiopia, the cradle of Rastafarians, of which reggae is an offshoot. Its specialty is pasta arrabbiata, which is penne pasta in a spicy tomato sauce with seared zucchini and yellow squash (providing red, green and gold, the colors associated with reggae). Also, RAGBRAIers gobble up marinated turkey tenderloins and smoked turkey drumsticks at Tender Tom's Turkey.

The most famous vendor traveling with RAGBRAI is Mr. Pork Chop. In 1983, Paul Bernhard, a hog farmer and former mayor of Bancroft, began setting up large grills along the route every morning, grilling inch-thick pork chops over corncob fires. They are served without plate or utensils, just a paper towel.

Overall, RAGBRAI's most popular food stop is not one that was created for the ride or travels with the cyclists. It's the HyVee, a chain of large, friendly grocery stores known to cater to RAGBRAI. From years of experience, it knows that riders will seek air conditioning, a place that will not run out of food (as many restaurants do)—and pasta. HyVee has plenty of all three. In overnight towns, it converts its grocery stores into makeshift restaurants by taking down food displays and installing tables. It beefs up the staff in its delicatessen and keeps its food court open until midnight instead of the usual 9:00 p.m. And the twenty-four-hour stores are open for late-nighters as well as those who hit the blacktop before dawn, as many riders do to beat the heat.

Unphased by the hungry, demanding RAGBRAI XL crowds, Ric Anderson, manager of the Marshalltown HyVee, says, "There's no downside to RAGBRAI. We increased our sales by 50 percent and smaller stores doubled their sales."

It helps that he has ridden RAGBRAI and that this was his fifth RAGBRAI with HyVee, three of them as the manager of a store. Plus, HyVee supports cycling by sponsoring an annual one-hundred-mile ride for juvenile diabetes. Four hundred employees, family and friends rode in 2012—not as many as the number who ride RAGBRAI but enough to help the company and some of its employees see RAGBRAI from the riders' perspective. "We hope there will always be a HyVee in every RAGBRAI town," Anderson says.

There are many lesser-known vendors, and every year hundreds of local professional and amateur cooks set up shop in or between the towns. In 2001, Vilma Woodke of Schaller made seven hundred lumpia with sweet-and-sour sauce using recipes from her native Philippines.

HyVee trucks and grocery stores are prominent throughout RAGBRAI. Open twenty-four-hours a day, the stores are popular with cyclists, who like a place that does not run out of food, as many restaurants do.

Prices are typically fair and reasonable. RAGBRAI is not Great America, where you're a captive customer of a corporate enterprise. In 1977, the Commercial Club of Mapleton sold a hot dog, sack of chips, cookies and a cold drink for a grand total of twenty-five cents. In the mid-1980s you could cross the state on about ten dollars a day for food. Today, about thirty-five would suffice.

Helping you stay on budget is the free food that was more common in the early years but still pops up occasionally. In 2012, Vital Ministries sliced up and handed out one thousand watermelons for free.

Finding a balance between feeding everyone and not having tons of leftovers is tricky. Fayette, one of the smallest overnight towns ever, was worried that it would not have enough food for RAGBRAIers in 1996. But it didn't want to go overboard, either. "I hope we do run out of food…as soon as everyone is fed," said Mike Simon, food committee co-chair. In any event, RAGBRAI leftovers don't go to waste. They usually get fed to the hogs.

THE WEATHER

Iowa's weather can be turbulent. Blizzards and winds out of the Rocky Mountains meet cooler winds from Canada and warmer air from the Gulf of Mexico. The result is constant, sometimes sudden change. The busiest, most watched instrument in the state just might be the thermometer.

Whether they see that thermometer as half full or half empty, cyclists are preoccupied with the weather forecast. How hot will it get? Will it rain? Which way will the wind blow? These are not idle questions related to convenience and comfort. For cyclists and campers exposed to the weather all day and night, their answers have the potential to inflict misery on the ride, prevent a good night's sleep, damage electronic equipment, breed illness and cause injury.

Workers, volunteers and organizers in host communities are also preoccupied with the forecast since rain, wind and extreme heat can wreak havoc on plans to serve food, entertain riders and raise money. And these communities have only a short period of time to make or break their goals and recoup their investments in food, supplies, personnel, overtime, insurance, etc. One day in 2000, heavy rain flooded many concession stands in Ankeny. Riders spent much of the day waiting in shelters for the rain to stop and then biking ahead as far as possible until rain recommenced. As a result, vendors in Mitchellville and Colfax sold hardly anything. By the time riders got to Pella, however, the rain had stopped, so that town enjoyed a windfall.

There's a saying on RAGBRAI: "You know you haven't lost the route if you face a headwind." This was certainly the case on "Saggy Thursday" in 1995, when the headwind was so strong that cyclists had to pedal to go *downhill*. The other most difficult day, weather-

Riders have learned to take rain in stride. *Janet Kersey Kowal.*

wise, was "Soggy Monday" in 1981, when daylong rain and cold left riders feeling miserable. "All I wanted to do was to get out of my wet clothes and into a dry martini," Kaul wrote.

Camping in severe weather is tough, too. All too common are stories of wind blowing away tents, rain soaking sleeping bags and humidity keeping campers up all night. The first night in 1999, before anyone had biked a mile, blaring tornado sirens sent campers scurrying to emergency shelters.

When the weather turns too good, however, hardcore RAGBRAIers complain about having nothing to complain about. As Karras put it on the second day of 1977, "If something doesn't happen soon to give this crowd something to crab about, I don't want to be around when we get to Lansing [the endpoint]. I can hear them already. 'What's the big deal,' they'll say. "You call this a bike ride? Kids stuff!'"

THE HILLS

Many cyclists learn the hard way that RAGBRAI is one *hill* of a ride. "When did Iowa grow hills?" one rider grumbled. Well, twelve thousand to forty thousand years ago, when glaciers advanced through the region.

"I like hills, especially the side that goes up," John Karras wrote. *Photo by Bob Frank, PBV.*

Other than the weather and food, RAGBRAIers talk more about hills than anything else. Some hate them and will never "get over it." Others are philosophical, such as the woman who said, "This day has been a metaphor for my life: one hill after another," and the man who happily accepted hill climbing because "what goes up must come down."

Some riders, such as those on Team Hills Angels, like the hills. In 1976, twelve-year-old Mark Beane complained to the *Register* that there weren't enough hills that year. (Indeed, the average climb per day was significantly less than it had been the previous two years.) And in 2012, many cyclists went out of their way to test themselves on School Hill, a 0.2-mile climb with a 20 to 26 percent grade, paying five dollars to Lehigh's Betterment Committee to be timed.

After hearing one too many complaints about hills, Karras once groused, "Anyone who doesn't like hills can go bike in Nebraska."

Love them or hate them, Iowa's hills endow each ride with great scenery and offer vantage points for admiring the countryside. They vary the ride and help avoid monotony. Also, without hills, riders wouldn't have the chance to coast and recover. Plus, hills provide material for endless jokes. A series of three, well-spaced signs up a steep hill in 2009 said: "You're over 40." "You're not over the hill." "Yet."

THE ACCOMMODATIONS

Most riders and their support staff camp in the main campgrounds provided by RAGBRAI or in campgrounds secured by their team, club or charter in parks, at schools or on fairgrounds. More and more, however, participants seek sleeping accommodations in private homes.

Some teams and clubs arrange for camping at private residences, such as the home of Tim and Becky Brelje of Harlan, where C.U.B.S. camped in 2008. That way they meet locals and get access to indoor plumbing. *Photo by Dave McWhinnie.*

RAGBRAI

Home stays started informally as early as the second or third year when rain, wind or heat drove would-be campers to seek shelter by knocking on doors. It turned out that many locals were, indeed, willing to open their basements or rec rooms to weary cyclists seeking a break from the elements. RAGBRAI began establishing a housing committee in each overnight town to match riders seeking a home stay with locals willing to put them up.

In 2008, Tipton's housing committee talked Ina Hack's daughter into volunteering her mother's house for two RAGBRAIers. Hack had never hosted before. She didn't have anything against the ride; she was simply too busy. Then ninety years old, she belonged to six bridge clubs, bowled once a week and biked around town. The visit worked out, but Hack did not see much of her guests; she spent all day giving tours, greeting cyclists and serving dinner at her church.

Another year, Marilyn and Marlin Perdue selected Kaye and Carter LeBeau from a Chamber of Commerce list of people seeking a home stay because they were attracted by their French name. The Perdues welcomed the LeBeaus with champagne and fois gras, but the LeBeaus are not French. Nonetheless, the two couples hit it off so well that the following month they went to France together for a week.

Thousands of Iowans open their hearts and homes to RAGBRAI every year. Barb and Marv Carpenter of Webster City hosted Kathy Schubert in 2012. *Photo by Kathy Schubert.*

Many individuals secure home stays on their own. Some lean on family and friends, and professionals are known to ask their counterparts in overnight towns for a spare bedroom. Kathy Schubert, who rides on her own, has elevated the search for a home stay to an art. Riding with her dog, Schubert has stayed with dog lovers who were found with the help of local veterinarians. She volunteers for the Red Cross and has found housing through local affiliates. And sometimes people with her same last name let her stay with them, even though they're not related.

Some teams line up indoor accommodations for their members or at least their leaders. Others who plan to camp in backyards hope their hosts will allow them to sleep indoors if the weather turns sour. Small groups and families often sleep in buses or recreational vehicles.

A big part of the search for accommodations involves RAGBRAI's hottest commodity: a hot shower. Old-timers brag that they used to shower with a garden hose—or not at all. Michael Leo, co-founder of the Tall Dog Bike Club, tells about a meeting in the 1970s when RAGBRAI coordinator Jim Green asked for ideas of how to improve the ride. When a young woman stood up and asked for hot showers, she was booed! "She wanted all the comforts of home, but that wasn't going to happen—or so it was thought at the time," Leo says.

Home stays usually guarantee a hot shower, but camping usually means waiting in line for a lukewarm shower, sometimes at a nearby school or YMCA. Some teams carry bags for shower water, setting them out in the sun to heat up during the day and providing makeshift shower stalls in the campsite. Team Dawg connected its shower stalls to a gas grill jerry-rigged with copper piping to heat the water. Such makeshift showers worked fine until recently, when some towns started to prohibit wastewater runoff.

RAGBRAIers have shown creativity in their perennial search for hot showers. They have showered in a number of unexpected places: funeral homes, school bus garages, fire stations, dorms and carwashes. Whatever it takes! Mike Benge suspects he and other members of Adaptive Sports Iowa, a team for disabled athletes, have had the best showers on RAGBRAI. "Once we stayed in a nursing home, and its showers had special doors, multiple nozzles you could spray at different angles and a seat you could tilt in different directions," he says.

The self-contained campers have it the roughest. They have to fend for themselves for both showers and a place to pitch their tents. They're a tough lot, often on a tight budget and heavily loaded with gear. In 2000, Deb Benton-Gevock and Kenny Gevock carried seventy-five pounds of bags on each of their bikes. BAGBRAI, anyone?

RAGBRAI timeline

1967
▷ John Karras buys a ten-speed.

1967–1973
▷ Karras and Donald Kaul get into distance cycling.

1973
▷ Karras and Kaul lead the Great Six-Day Bike Ride Across Iowa.
▷ U.S. bicycle boom peaks; 15 million bikes sold.

1974
▷ Second ride occurs, but with a different route and an earlier start.
▷ Karras creates "instant tradition" of dipping rear wheel in Missouri River and front wheel in Mississippi River.

1975
▷ Long-term name adopted: RAGBRAI followed by a Roman numeral.
▷ RAGBRAI already tries to limit the size of the ride, but to no avail.

1977
▷ Shortest (379 miles) and flattest (10,675 feet) ride ever.
▷ RAGBRAI "goes to college," camping at Luther College in Decorah.

1980
▷ *Register*'s editor writes an article portraying RAGBRAI as lewd. Riders respond with raucous, dangerous party in Elkader.

1981
▷ "Soggy Monday:" rain all day and temperatures in the forties.

1982
▷ RAGBRAI fixes the date of the ride as the last full week of July.
▷ Kaul retires.
▷ RAGBRAI introduces a drawing for registrants and a fee ($12.50) for riding.

1983
▷ Clarence Pickard Memorial Ride.
▷ Chuck Offenburger becomes co-host and rides his first RAGBRAI.

1984
▷ The ride overnights in Shenandoah, Offenburger's hometown.
▷ RAGBRAI first death: Mark Knief dies from heart attack while cycling.

1985
▷ Longest ride ever (550 miles).

1986
▷ Optional "century loop" instituted.
▷ RAGBRAI introduces ID wristbands.
▷ First presumed presidential candidate, Bruce Babbitt, rides RAGBRAI.

1987
▷ Karras misses ride due to heart attack.

1988
▷ RAGBRAI returns to Des Moines for the first time.

1989
▷ RAGBRAI introduces sponsorship program. First to sign up: Miller's Brewing Co., Nike, Farmland Foods, Champion Grove and the University of Iowa.
▷ Someone throws nails on the route.

1991
▷ Don Benson retires as coordinator; Jim Green takes over.

1993
▷ "Flood of the Century" inflicts "water torture" on Iowa.

1995
▷ "Saggy Thursday:" thousands sag due to hills, ninety-five-degree heat and headwind.

1996
▷ Iowa's cross-country sesquicentennial bike ride includes RAGBRAI.

1997
▷ Ride goes through Lucas County, the last of Iowa's ninety-nine counties to be included.
▷ Someone throws thumbtacks on the route.

1998
▷ Offenburger leaves the *Register*.
▷ Ride finishes in tiny Sabula, Iowa's only island town.

1999
▷ First RAGBRAI Expo of vendors, bike shops and others.
▷ *RAGBRAI: Everyone Pronounces It Wrong* by John and Ann Karras is published.

2000
▷ Karras retires as co-host. Brian Duffy signs on.

2001
▷ The optional century loop is named the John Karras Loop.

2002
▷ Remembrance ride for the tragedies of September 11, 2001.

2003
▷ Cycling legend Greg LeMond participates.

2004
▷ Cyclist Kirk Ullrich is thrown from his bike after his wheel gets caught in a centerline crack. His widow sues Crawford county.
▷ Green retires, and T.J. Juskiewicz takes over as director.

2006
▷ Lance Armstrong participates. (He would return in '07, '08 and '11.)

2007
▷ In response to the lawsuit concerning Ullrich's death, Crawford Country bans RAGBRAI to avoid liability.

2008
▷ Crawford County rescinds its ban on RAGBRAI.

2010
▷ RAGBRAI institutes annual Route Announcement Party to reveal the top-secret overnight towns and ending town.

2012
▷ Fortieth-anniversary bash honors seven cyclists who biked every year.

Chapter 4

RAGBRAI CATCHES ON, GROWS

The Benson Years

Turning back to the history of the ride, let's recall that John Karras and Donald Kaul had proposed the first cross-state ride as a lark and had no intention of repeating the feat. Still, the ride was fun, in a crazy way, and no one got hurt. After the *Register* received bin loads of letters asking for an encore, the paper decided to organize another ride and dubbed it the Second Annual Great Bicycle Ride Across Iowa (SAGBRAI).

The year 1974 turned out to be a watershed, setting precedents and shaping future RAGBRAIs.

- Obvious but vital, the second route was different from the first. Inadvertently, this ensured that each future ride would be distinctive and that, overall, RAGBRAI would eventually engage the entire state.
- The starting date was moved earlier to accommodate teachers and students who were unable to join the first ride because their schools were already in session.
- The ride was lengthened from six to seven days to allow for fewer miles each day and routes with more zigzags.
- The Iowa State Patrol stepped up to handle traffic safety.
- Don "Wagonmaster" Benson, in the *Register*'s promotion department, took over logistics. He ironed out problems that plagued the first ride, organizing sag wagons, baggage trucks and medical assistance. Also, he worked with host communities and established the practice of driving the route beforehand to see if it was suitable.
- Karras invented the "instant tradition" of dipping your rear wheel in the Missouri River (or one of its tributaries) at the start of the ride and dipping your front wheel in the Mississippi River at the end. He later described the tradition as "balderdash," but it stuck.

Members of Team Gourmet dip their wheels in the Mississippi River in 2005, an "instant tradition" fabricated by John Karras out of thin air in 1974. *Janet Kersey Kowal.*

The turnout for SAGBRAI was tremendous. About 2,700 cyclists showed up in Council Bluffs, the starting town, and an estimated 1,700 cyclists rode all the way to Dubuque. Clearly there was strong and growing interest in this "nutty" idea. Year two involved more camping, since the overnight towns did not have nearly enough hotel rooms to accommodate the larger number of cyclists.

One thing SAGBRAI did not establish for future RAGBRAIs was clothing styles. In the early years, cyclists wore cutoffs, tennis shoes and T-shirts; today, RAGBRAI's easy riders wear padded shorts, cleated shoes and micro-fiber jerseys that wick away perspiration.

With more time to plan and anticipate the entrepreneurial opportunities that RAGBRAI presented, locals prepared food and drink for sale. Although the participants were clearly at the mercy of locals, the Iowans did not gouge the riders. In Atlantic, the first overnight stop, the Kiwanis Club served ham and cheese sandwiches, baked beans, tossed salad, potato chips and coffee or iced tea for $1.75. A rider who had moved from Florida to Iowa told the *Register,* "I can't believe it. If you tried to do this in Florida, everybody would be trying to rip you off."

A few groups continued the practice of serving riders for free. Each member of the Better Elk Horn Club in the pass-through town of Elk Horn provided four-dozen cookies, enough to give one cookie to each rider. In Kimballton, the Progressive Danes gave away thirty cases of free soda. Mertyle Hansen, a member of the community club, said, "We didn't want to make money at this. We just wanted the people to come here."

"The natives were friendly," Kaul wrote. The cyclists showed their appreciation by being polite, tidy and fun. They built up a reputation for leaving their campgrounds as clean as they found them.

Creativity, unpredictability and goofiness defined the carefree ride. Campers sang folk songs, played Frisbee and did other things that were popular in the 1970s. On Monday afternoon of SAGBRAI, a light plane circled the campground and a small parachute appeared in the sky. Written on the parachute was "Airmail letter for Gene Angove," and attached to the parachute was a bottle with a message inside.

Some hardy souls rode their bikes to the start, as if seven days of heat and hills were not enough. One of them was John Steger from Dyersville in northeastern Iowa. "I missed the trip last year so I thought I'd better do it both ways this time," he said.

Iowa's cornfields make up the world's largest outhouses. Farmers often put out toilet paper and joke that their crop yields increase in the year that RAGBRAI passes through. *Photo by Bob Frank.*

One significant step in 1974 was the decision to test whether a small town could function as well as a medium-size town as an overnight stop. True, the first ride had included Williamsburg, with a population of 1,544, but the riders numbered in the low hundreds in 1973 rather than in the thousands, as they did in 1974. Guthrie Center, with a population of 1,834, was selected for the test. It would be the first overnight town where the number of cyclists exceeded the number of residents.

Despite some initial trepidation, the people of Guthrie Center were extremely welcoming. For their part, the cyclists were gracious and courteous. "It could be argued that we discovered RAGBRAI there, because everyone—townspeople and bicyclists alike—had the time of their lives," Karras wrote later. After that, RAGBRAI never hesitated to overnight in small towns.

SAGBRAI still left room for improvement and better coordination among all parties. Shower facilities were woefully inadequate. Freshly oiled asphalt along the planned route outside of Waterloo required a last-minute detour. And most bathrooms, even some *towns*, ran out of toilet paper.

On the last day, about five thousand cyclists and greeters accompanied by more than one thousand cars, trucks, campers and buses assembled in Dubuque's Eagle Point Park to celebrate the "glorious" completion of the ride. And they were already clamoring for another ride the following year.

1975

The third ride added more touches to the event, further defining it for years to come, starting with the name. SAGBRAI was fine for year two, but no one looked forward to TAGBRAI, FAGBRAI or NAGBRAI. After the *Register*'s editor suggested that the newspaper's name should be part of the title, Karras came up with what he calls "a silly acronym that could go the distance": RAGBRAI followed by a Roman numeral.

RAGBRAI III underscored the newly established commitment to small towns by selecting Hawarden (population 2,789 and falling) as its starting point, a job that is more demanding on local goodwill and facilities than serving as simply an overnight town. No one knew whether such a small town was up to the job.

Hawarden was ready, but the roads to the east of it were not. On day one, riders approaching Cherokee were appalled to come across a long section of road repaved the day before with tar and little red rocks. "In a matter of moments, the RAGBRAI army, already 4,000 strong, was transformed into a motley band of stragglers, bikes stained with tar, tires glued with rocks, walking their bikes," Kaul wrote. They had been tarred and pebbled! One more lesson learned—the hard way—for the still novice RAGBRAI officials.

The early RAGBRAIs had only one sag wagon, pulled by a Massey-Ferguson tractor. *Kaye and Carter LeBeau.*

1976–1979

There were many more lessons learned the hard way. In 1976, a sandbur-strewn campground caused hundreds of flat tires. In 1979, at least eight cyclists were thrown from their bikes when their wheels got caught in centerline cracks in one stretch of road near Churdan. Meanwhile, drivers occasionally took exception with RAGBRAI for taking up the road. In 1979, truck driver Michael Whelan was chased down by the highway patrol and fined $290 for speeding, improper passing, reckless driving and failure to yield to an emergency vehicle. "It's not known if he now likes RAGBRAI any better," Karras quipped.

On a more positive note, in 1977 and 1978, college campuses (Luther College and Cornell College, respectively) proved to be great sites for RAGBRAI to visit and camp. And many observers noted that bicycle helmets were becoming increasingly common. Both trends boded well. In addition, 1977 was the shortest (379 miles) and flattest (10,675 feet of climbing) ride, before or since—something that encouraged more participation.

Before RAGBRAI was known throughout the state, many towns were not prepared for what was increasingly characterized as a horde of locusts, devouring everything in

The *Register*'s baggage truck in Lansing at the end of RAGBRAI V. *Steve Kobberdahl.*

sight. To help restaurants cope with the crowds, RAGBRAIers often pitched in, cooking and performing other tasks. Rider Greg Schmidt took over the Urbana Café's grill on RAGBRAI VI, and it wasn't the first time he had helped cook. "Usually you try to train another rider to take over when you're ready to go or they won't let you leave," he said.

During these years, local residents established the tradition of going all out to welcome and entertain riders. The Clear Lake girls' basketball cheerleaders gave away popcorn. Sacred Heart Church in Laurens held a polka mass. When the campgrounds flooded in Rockwell City in 1977, local residents took campers into their homes. And on and on.

Benson, who would continue as coordinator until 1991, "imposed order on chaos," as many have put it. "He was an organizing genius and a great detail man," Karras says. He improved the planning, organization and logistical processes that helped the ride grow, all the while ensuring the safety of riders.

From no safety officers, no medical crews and only one bike shop owner the first year, by 1979 RAGBRAI had local police, sheriffs, thirteen state troopers, five rescue vehicles and fifteen bike shops working the entire ride. And once the growing number of private, rider-support vehicles along the route began to constitute a safety hazard, Benson instituted a vehicle route and banned those vehicles from the bike route.

In the meantime, cyclists found that there was, indeed, safety in numbers. For once, they had the upper hand on their nemesis: dogs. As thousands of cyclists ride by on RAGBRAI, dogs along the way seem shell-shocked, unable to take up the chase, as they are wont to do.

1980–1982

In 1980, *Register* editor Michael Gartner wrote a scathing article portraying RAGBRAI as a sex and drug scene (see the chapter "Shift Happens"). That led to a raucous night in Elkader at the end of RAGBRAI VIII, but the ride rebounded the following year without any apparent ill effects.

The ride in 1981 established once and for all that Mother Nature was in charge. Day one was rainy. On day two, the rain worsened, the temperature fell into the upper forties and a strong headwind kicked in. Fewer than half of the riders made it past the first town, nineteen miles in. This turned out to be RAGBRAI's worst day of weather, before or since. It was so cold that riders passing through Schleswig descended on a men's clothing store that was having a sale and cleaned it out. The rain did not let up throughout the day, and riders became increasingly wretched and despondent. Kaul later wrote, "Why did God choose me to die of hypothermia on a July day in Iowa?" Local residents helped rescue the wretched riders in cars, pickups, flatbeds, hay wagons and cattle trucks in scenes resembling the Allied evacuation at Dunkirk.

That evening, Lake City locals went to great lengths to alleviate the misery. They took in, dried off and cleaned up the riders, sheltering them in homes, garages and schools. Those who rode the whole day—heck, anyone who was there—would tell stories about the hardship, comparing what later became known as "Soggy Monday" with World War I. Kaul compared it to Moby Dick: "You expected some bearded guy with a harpoon to come running out of a farmyard yelling: 'Thar she blows!'" After Monday, the weather turned nice for the rest of the week.

Also in 1981, seven cyclists fell on a gravel road at the bottom of a steep hill. That same year, significant thefts of wallets and other personal possessions were reported for the first time.

The weather was gentle the following year, almost too gentle. "This ride has been cooled by clouds, kissed by breezes, warmed by the sun and lemonaded and cookied half to death," Karras wrote midway through the week. "First-timers are getting the wrong impression about this event. Unless things get bad fast, they're going to end the ride in Davenport thinking this is supposed to be fun."

That same year, Clarence Pickard, folk hero of the first ride, was killed at the age of ninety-two by a car while crossing the street in his hometown of Indianola. The following RAGBRAI was dubbed the Clarence Pickard Memorial Ride.

By this time, newspapers had already begun their inexorable decline. In 1982, the *Register* lost money for the first time in one quarter, so it declared that all promotions would have to pay their way. Costing the paper about $10,000 a year, RAGBRAI had to institute a registration fee to recover its expenses. It was set at $12.50. At the same time, the *Register* promised that money left over would be donated to charitable and community organizations across Iowa, a practice it continues to this day.

RAGBRAI fixed the date of the ride henceforth as the last full week of July. For the first time, RAGBRAI designated official radio stations along the route to provide news about the ride, emergencies and the weather.

At the end of RAGBRAI X, co-founder Donald Kaul announced, "pleading sanity," that ten years of RAGBRAI was enough for him. "All we planned was a bicycle ride, not a life sentence," he said. Readers and riders alike would miss his wit.

From the start, he had a love-hate relationship with the ride. After the first ride, he wrote, "I don't care if I never see a bicycle again. By 'never' I mean three days."

On the folly of RAGBRAI: "Anyone who sets out to spend the day sitting on a bicycle seat, which is shaped like a flat iron and is about as soft, deserves what he gets."

On RAGBRAI's rapid growth: "If RAGBRAI gets any bigger, we'll have to stay in one location and let the towns come to us."

On RAGBRAI VIII: "There's a bright side to this. If I perish on the road I won't have to go on RAGBRAI IX."

On why he always rode in the back of the pack: "You don't see generals rushing into battle at the head of their troops anymore. They hang back to plan things, oversee matters and shoot stragglers."

1983–1984

Chuck Offenburger, the *Register*'s "Iowa Boy" columnist, took over as co-host, although he had never ridden RAGBRAI and had not owned a bike until three weeks before the ride started. Offenburger attacked his new assignment with, as he put it, a banana in one pocket and rosary in the other. "Stop me on the trip and say hello, or give me a scoop," he wrote. "You won't have any trouble picking me out…I'm the tubby guy from Shenandoah wearing lawn-mowing clothes on his first real bike ride." His new bike, on the other hand, had enough gears "to ride up your garage wall," said Forrest Ridgway, the owner of Bike World, who sold it to him. Right off the bat, Offenburger admitted that he would do RAGBRAI the "pantywaist way," i.e., staying in air-conditioned motels every night.

Karras picked up where he had left off with Kaul and started ribbing Offenburger, "a callow upstart." The new kid took ribbing from other quarters, too. One church along the route sold "Offenburgers made of ground Chuck."

One of the perks of being co-host is steering RAGBRAI to your hometown, but that was not as easy as Offenburger thought it would be. When he accompanied Benson and Karras to Shenandoah in 1984 to announce the idea to his friends, the Chamber of Commerce's executive director balked.

"How quickly do you need an answer?"

"Now," Benson answered.

"Oh, I don't have the authority," the director said. "I'll have to get the board together, and that could take a week."

While Karras and Benson glared at recently minted co-host Offenburger, supposedly one of Shenandoah's favorite sons, Benson told the director, "If you don't say 'yes' right now, we're driving to Clarinda and giving it to them."

Pause. "Shenandoah would be honored to host RAGBRAI XII," the director said.

On the same route selection trip, the first word out of the mouth of an official in Pella when he heard that his town had been selected as an overnight spot on RAGBRAI was, "Shit!" Offenburger recounts.

Such was the apprehension about hosting RAGBRAI, even thirteen years after it had begun. People didn't know what to make of it. But they learned. In 1982, RAGBRAI was thought to be worth about $100,000 in revenue to an overnight town, and that figure grew considerably over the years.

In 1984, the inevitable happened. Mark Knief, a twenty-eight-year-old with a heart condition, died of a heart attack at the top of a steep hill. It's remarkable that no one had ever died before on RAGBRAI, given the number of participants. Then, another death occurred later in the week. Thirty-year-old Janet Newell disappeared, and her body was later found drowned in the Des Moines River. The death was never solved, but no foul play was suspected. Benson said RAGBRAI was shaken by these deaths. "These people are part of one big family, and you become close to them even though you don't know them."

Offenburger ferreted out colorful RAGBRAI stories over the next several years. He found the "biggest" plumber in Wright County, a six-foot, five-inch man who weighed 310 pounds, who was cleaning out a sewer line blocked by the thousands of RAGBRAIers. "Some things you can't plan for, like how a forty-year-old sewer line is going to behave with nonstop traffic," Lee Lunde said. "But we can fix a plugged sewer. Bring 'em all back to see us!"

"Iowa Boy" also started a RAGBRAI poetry committee. He lamented the many abandoned Rock Island Railroad depots across Iowa that were evident along the ride. And he started a T-shirt derby, noting everything from "It takes two to tandem" to "Dubuque or puke" the year the ride ended in that charming town. (Some T-shirts that could have won the derby in later years include: "Estimated time of arrival? Oh, who cares!"; "Hey Lance, on your left"; "I spent 7 days behind bars," below an image of bicycle handlebars; and "Ride your bike!—God.")

RAGBRAI

Karras devoted much of his daily missives to recognizing the participation of every club, church and cause involved. He tried to list them all but never could because there were more than one hundred some days. "I think I can say without fear of contradiction that I'm the 'champeen' chronicler of cookie and lemonade stands in the Western Hemisphere. No, in the world," he wrote.

Not only did RAGBRAI provide grist for reporters and columnists, but it also helped fill the paper by generating scores of letters to the editor. Most were positive, but several motorists resented RAGBRAI for taking over the road. "I propose that RAGBRAI bikers carry a copy of safety rules and be required to follow them on the 'great ride,' just as they would be expected to in their hometown on an ordinary ride," wrote Linda Meyer of Indianola in 1984.

1985

Such a casual attitude toward safety was not the cause of RAGBRAI's first traffic fatality. In 1985, cyclist Charles Kithcart was walking down the sidewalk in Emmetsburg when a driver lost control of her van, which jumped the curb and struck him.

During the mid-1980s, Iowa was suffering from drought conditions and a farm-debt crisis. Some suggested that RAGBRAI be cancelled out of concern for farmers, but the ride continued unabated. Organizers realized that the interactions it fostered engendered a better understanding of what it means to be a farmer.

Perhaps because 1984 had been an easy year for riders, RAGBRAI officials made the ride in 1985 tough. At 550 miles, it remains the longest ever. Iowa is 310 miles across, so how could the ride be so long? By zigzagging across the state. The rationale for doing this in 1985 was to accommodate as many as possible of the more than forty communities that had asked to participate. "If it had not been for favorable tailwinds the last four days, RAGBRAI XIII would have been a disaster," RAGBRAI officials later admitted. There will probably never be a longer RAGBRAI, although riders have kidded Karras about secretly wishing for a 700-mile ride, made up of seven century rides.

In 1985, Karras took good-natured revenge on Offenburger, "that RAGBRAI newcomer," by staging his own "triumphant return" to his hometown, as "Iowa Boy" had done in Shenandoah in 1984. The only problem was that Karras is from Cleveland. Therefore, he asked small towns in Iowa to adopt him. After several volunteered, he chose Humbolt, which outdid itself in welcoming back its "favorite son."

The two RAGBRAI co-hosts had to cooperate on the basketball court in the first of many challenge games against local stars. Nevertheless, they usually lost. This year they got clobbered two-on-two in Ventura and Waterloo—by girls. OK, the girls were high school basketball stars, but still.

Some years are tougher than others. Here, in 2009, riders find that shade and water provide the perfect rest stop. *Ken Urban Photography.*

Two biplanes flew above the course all week, jazzing up the bike ride with an air show. RAGBRAI veteran Gary Lust piloted one of the planes and performed stunts for the cyclists, who included his family.

Meanwhile, RAGBRAI continued to grow by leaps and bounds. By the mid-1980s, the ride attracted as many as twenty thousand participants some days. Growing national media attention contributed to this, and a sizeable press corps began to travel with RAGBRAI.

1986

RAGBRAI introduced ID wristbands to clarify who had registered and was therefore eligible for RAGBRAI services. Of course, medical crews were not going to start leaving bleeding cyclists along the side of the road, but sag wagon services were available only to registered riders. In addition, Benson threatened to conduct wristband checks outside showers and kybos that were provided by RAGBRAI. With the introduction of wristbands, RAGBRAI renewed its call for participants to register and pay their fees in order to support the services.

Another change this year was instituting an optional century loop. Each of the previous seven years had included a crushing yet mandatory one-hundred-mile (or nearly) day. Making the century optional encouraged families and inexperienced riders to try RAGBRAI while allowing hardcore riders to push themselves and earn additional bragging rights.

By the mid-1980s, commercial interests were encroaching on RAGBRAI. A few corporate names had been bandied about in previous years, but in 1986 some companies garnered official recognition. Northwestern Bell and General Telephone were recognized for providing enhanced telecommunications. And Godfather's Pizza sold pizza along the route and provided "fanny bumpers," small placards to be placed on the back of bikes with the name and hometown of the rider, along with Godfather's name.

Karras, himself a principal RAGBRAI decision maker, questioned Godfather's presence, writing that it "threatens part of what has made RAGBRAI so appealing to so many"—that is, the local vendors who add color and charm. "How could the Altar and Rosary Society or the local 4-H club compete against corporate giants? Of course, they couldn't. Shortly they would stop trying. And that, friends, would be the end of RAGBRAI."

Something else disturbed Karras and others this year: the first participation by a possible presidential candidate, Bruce Babbitt. Karras envisioned several candidates clogging up the road with security forces and media minions, compounding safety concerns. "RAGBRAI is enough of a circus without adding another ring," he wrote. His concerns about the corporatization of RAGBRAI turned out to be more founded than those about the politicalization of RAGBRAI.

1987–1988

As it turns out, Karras had bigger things to worry about. He suffered a heart attack a few days before RAGBRAI XV. His wife, Ann, RAGBRAI veteran from the beginning and co-author with John of *RAGBRAI: Everyone Pronounces It Wrong*, worked the ride on his behalf. During the week, John wrote one piece for the *Register* from his sick bed, referring to this ride as RAGBRAI XIVb, saying that "Grandpa RAGBRAI" could not fathom an official ride without him.

Whatever it was called, RAGBRAI still had plenty of firsts up its sleeve. It celebrated Thanksgiving in Little Turkey, a pass-through town of sixteen inhabitants that served turkey sandwiches. (The town takes its name from the nearby Little Turkey River.) The University of Northern Iowa offered a weeklong, one-credit, evening course in astronomy during RAGBRAI. And Ben Davidson, an Oakland Raiders star and Miller Lite television pitchman, rode for the first of many times. With a booming

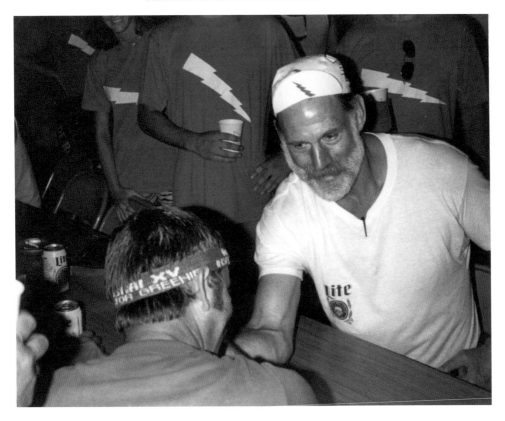

Ben Davidson, former Oakland Raiders defensive end and then Miller Lite pitchman, unwinds on his first RAGBRAI in 1987. *Kaye and Carter LeBeau.*

voice, the six-foot, eight-inch Davidson stood out, especially when he walked into a bar and bought a round for everyone, using Miller Brewing Co.'s pocket money.

The year was marred by another death. John Boyle, nineteen, was crushed under the wheels of a truck passing in the opposite direction. Boyle lost control of his bike as he was riding in a pace line on the left side of the road. This was RAGBRAI's first fatality resulting from a collision between a motor vehicle and someone actually riding a bicycle.

Two weeks before the next ride began, someone discovered that no one had signed up from Rhode Island. This meant that RAGBRAI could not boast of having a rider from all fifty states, as it had done for the previous five years. Therefore, a drawing was held in that distant state. Malcolm Starr won, and RAGBRAI flew him out, most expenses paid.

With the Iowa State Penitentiary in Fort Madison at the end of the ride, cyclists must have wondered whether RAGBRAI XVI was going to lead to a prison sentence. "If we behave reasonably well, there's a good chance for a pardon," because the governor, Terry Branstad, planned to ride, Offenburger wrote.

RAGBRAI

This year was notable for returning to Des Moines for the first time since year one. How would the state's largest city stack up to the now legendary small-town hospitality? The reception began the night before in Boone when riders were issued summons to appear in court the next day. In this case, "court" referred to the popular Court Avenue downtown entertainment district.

Arriving in Des Moines, riders rode over a red carpet between lampposts sporting eveningwear. Welcoming committees gave them paper bowties to dress up for the party. Some local residents grumbled about traffic tie-ups, and bikes were stolen. On the other hand, many residents took the day off to welcome the riders and participate in the festivities. An estimated twenty-five thousand people attended parties at many venues, draining 106 kegs of beer, 115 gallons of wine coolers (hey, it was the 1980s) and 105 gallons of lemonade schnapps—just along Court Avenue. Most riders camped nearby on the grounds of the state capitol, and some had a rough time turning out the next morning for the seventy-two-mile ride to Oskaloosa.

Karras, who had argued vociferously against overnighting in Des Moines due to fear about traffic tie-ups, bicycle thefts and out-of-control partying, happily ate crow the next day. All of these problems occurred, but less seriously than Karras had anticipated.

1989

This year didn't start off on such a positive note. Someone threw roofing nails along fourteen miles of the route north of Clarinda. County officials sent street sweepers, but not before dozens of early morning riders got one or more flats. With any luck, some of them were among the thirty-five riders picked at random for a lavish VIP picnic in Atlantic.

The big news this year was that RAGBRAI introduced a sponsorship program: partner for $10,000, associate for $5,000 and friend for $2,500. First on board were Miller Brewing Co., Champion Glove, Nike, Farmland Foods and the University of Iowa. How this would play out remained to be seen. But there was no denying that the ride was becoming a big business.

This year, ultra-marathon cyclist Bob Breedlove rode RAGBRAI for the first time, finishing it in thirty hours while burning off a liquid diet of thirty thousand calories. The year before, he had finished the six-thousand-mile Race Across America in ten days and twelve hours (seventh place). He would become a fixture on RAGBRAI.

Putting up with the many hills this year was worth it for baseball and movie fans who were keen on visiting the real Field of Dreams, made famous by the movie *Field of Dreams* and located a short distance outside Dyersville. A few miles away, art aficionados were treated to an original, $50,000 art project casting neon lights on 144 white tents at the University of Northern Iowa.

1990–1991

RAGBRAI XVIII got off to a "Sioux-per" start with free breakfast, a first that made some wonder why the ride had never started in Sioux Center before. Some people in this strongly religious community do not approve of conducting business on Sunday, so the town provided free breakfast for the first five thousand takers. In a somewhat related event, members of the Siouxland Christian Action Council lined the road on the first day of the ride holding signs against abortion. Council head Paul Dorr told the *Register* that the pickets "were not against RAGBRAI, but we wanted to make our point against abortion and the *Register*'s coverage of abortion."

More politicians came along each year. As rider Tom Tauke, an Iowa representative running for the U.S. Senate, put it during the send-off in Sioux Center, "There are two real ways to see Iowa; ride RAGBRAI or run for office."

Spencer provided an exhibition of "roller-blading," complete with one hundred pairs for riders to try. Popular in California for years, rollerblading was slow to reach Iowa. At least Iowa launched one nationwide trend: cross-state bicycle rides!

Readers were happy to see Kaul back on the ride for one year. He speculated that he had been called back because "the *Register* hasn't had any representation at the back of the ride" since he'd left eight years before. Kaul had not lost his touch, grousing about how RAGBRAI was like Pickett's Charge: "an undisciplined dash in pursuit of an uncertain objective, across ground that one can occupy but not own, to face certain defeat at the hands of superior forces: heat, wind, rain and crowded restrooms."

The weather cooperated most of the ride, but not Thursday night, when rain washed out most of Cedar Rapids' planned festivities. More than three hundred volunteers worked around the clock to blow up eighteen thousand balloons for a huge sculpture of a person riding a bike, but wind and rain destroyed the piece and battered riders. The foul weather continued until the end of the ride, giving Kaul just the excuse he was looking for not to ride. "I really enjoyed today's ride," he said at the closing ceremonies in Burlington. "It was in a Buick."

The next RAGBRAI started off with a bang, a volley of shots by buck-skinners with muzzleloading rifles. The festivities during the first twenty-four hours were representative of the whole week: local bands; bike races in Atlantic's business district; a VIP breakfast for a rider from each state, picked at random; and an outdoor Methodist service where the ministers, one of whom was a rider, presided from a hay rack.

The next day, riders were treated to welcome kisses, free massages, farm tours, a chat with a local resident who had witnessed a Bonnie and Clyde bank robbery in Stuart and John Wayne look-alike and sound-alike contests at his birth home in Winterset. "I can't remember a day with better stops," says veteran Carter LeBeau. "It was hard to make any time on the bike because the next stop was better than the last. It was a delight."

RAGBRAI

RAGBRAI XIX ended in Bellevue, where a downpour had ruined the ride's conclusion two years earlier. This time, the weather cooperated, and the closing ceremony turned into a salute to Benson, who was retiring as coordinator. He could be gruff and demanding. His friend Tim Lane once compared him with George Patton and Bobby Knight. Still, Benson nurtured RAGBRAI from its birth through adolescence.

Chapter 5

FURTHER DEVELOPMENT

The Green Years

1992

Jim Green, who worked in the *Register*'s circulation department, took over as coordinator in 1992 without missing a beat because he had been biking RAGBRAI since 1982, eight times as a way of drumming up circulation and engaging paperboys in competitions and promotions.

Right out of the block, however, Green was confronted with serious issues. In March, many residents of Glenwood expressed displeasure at having been selected as the starting point for RAGBRAI XX. Three years earlier, public and underage drinking had marred the event there. Also, the revelers had left behind a lot of trash and broken glass. "Does the perception that Glenwood is a good place for a two-day drunk to start RAGBRAI enhance the attractiveness of the city?" asked Jeff DeYoung, editor of the local *Opinion-Tribune*.

A month after that, an article in *Bicycling Magazine* portrayed RAGBRAI "through the bottom of a beer bottle." Co-host Chuck Offenburger was so troubled by RAGBRAI's checkered reputation that he wrote in a *Register* editorial, "I need to rethink my involvement."

At the same time, the Iowa State Patrol stepped forward and demanded better safety on RAGBRAI. "You've got one year to straighten things out, or we're pulling out," Green says the patrol told him. That prompted him to initiate Ride Right, a safety program. The title refers not only to riding correctly and courteously but also to riding on the right, having the right equipment and adopting the right attitude. Veteran Tim Lane, of Team Skunk, headed up the effort, and each host town formed a Ride Right committee.

Glenwood decided to give RAGBRAI another chance, and their event went well. One key was fencing in the beer garden. Police made a point by writing eighty-two

Bunching causes some bike crashes, but pace lines are the worst. *Photo by Bob Frank.*

alcohol-related tickets, and RAGBRAI XX got off to a sober start. Some riders resented the additional police presence and questioned RAGBRAI's commitment to moderation, noting that Miller Brewing Co. was a charter sponsor. Still, RAGBRAI officials appeared determined to clean up the ride.

These efforts succeeded in calming RAGBRAI down a bit. Kaul, back to help celebrate RAGBRAI's twentieth birthday, wrote, "It's not the Mormon Tabernacle Choir on wheels, but the ride remains wholesome."

In any event, 1992 was a rough year. There was reportedly too much drinking in the pass-through town of New Virginia, and several cyclists mooned the crowd. A rider was arrested in Des Moines for carrying a concealed knife. And a record thirty-five bikes were stolen, twenty of them in Des Moines. After realizing that partying had gotten out of control during RAGBRAI's last swing through Mount Pleasant eight years earlier, the town placed its beer garden next to the city jail.

Starting this year, riders were required to sign a waiver and release-from-liability form.

RAGBRAI had not overnighted in Marshalltown for eighteen years. The Iowa Valley Bicycle Club wanted the ride to come there in 1993, so Tom Kurth and fellow club members biked sixty-three miles to Des Moines and delivered a proposal to RAGBRAI in person. That was the first time anyone had done such a thing, so RAGBRAI officials were impressed. Nevertheless, Marshalltown was bypassed again in 1993. Undeterred, the club did the same thing the next year, and RAGBRAI finally visited Marshalltown in 1994.

1993

Early in the year, RAGBRAI staffers tried something new: biking one day of the ride beforehand as a test. They did this because they feared that the sixty-nine-mile ride from Decorah to Manchester was too hilly and difficult. (It wasn't.) In subsequent years, staffers expanded on the practice, adding days to the point where today they inspect the entire route by bike in June.

Iowa's "Flood of the Century" in the spring and summer of 1993 created a soaked and sodden state of affairs. Roads were impassable, campgrounds under water and the huge volunteer forces that RAGBRAI always depends on were working feverishly on flood-related issues. Many host towns couldn't get kybos because they were all needed elsewhere, especially in Des Moines, where the flooded waterworks left the capital city without running water for twelve days.

Should RAGBRAI be allowed to occur? Ironically, the only other time cancelling RAGBRAI was considered was due to the opposite situation, a drought in the 1980s.

Despite the flooding, state officials and RAGBRAI determined that the ride was needed more than ever to help lift spirits and generate income across the state. "Now is not the time, with all the tragedy in this state, to cancel an event that says so much about our spirit," said *Register* publisher Charlie Edwards. Besides, host communities had already invested heavily in the ride. So the ride proceeded, and cyclists were encouraged to contribute to flood relief efforts.

Kaul rode again but kept quiet until the end. Either he was getting soft or he simply enjoyed not having to file daily columns this time. In any event, he set aside his usual acerbic wit and wrote: "All in all, there's an essentially sweet, wholesome quality to the ride that is Iowa to the core. A few jerks aside, RAGBRAI is basically a Festival of Nice. The bikers are nice, the townspeople are nice and you come away from the experience feeling vaguely upbeat and optimistic about the human race.

"If I went on it more than once a year it would ruin my career," he couldn't resist adding.

When the ride is easy and the weather cooperates, RAGBRAI offers lots of free time to hang out in camp or participate in evening festivities. *Photo by Bob Frank, PBV.*

1994–1995

In 1994, the ride included a near record of fifty-five pass-through towns. One was an overnight in Perry, with a theme of "Perry-dise," which pretty much described the whole ride, one of the most pleasant ever, with near perfect weather and a tailwind.

But things did not go well for David Thomas, from Buffalo, New York, on his third RAGBRAI. Near the end of the ride he was using a kybo when someone pushed it over, covering Thomas with filth. Others came to his rescue, hosed him down and took him to get a shower. Thomas later found out that he had four broken ribs but remained philosophical. "I suppose that first morning right after it happened, I was thinking I'd never come back. But now? Sure, I'll be back next year," he told the *Register* in October. In fact, he returned to Iowa sooner than that. Maquoketa, the town where the incident had occurred, tried to make it right with him by flying him back for a special visit in December full of gifts, tours and meals.

RAGBRAI went online in 1995 with its own website. Another sign of the times was a survey revealing that 34 percent of riders planned to bring cellphones. RAGBRAI was losing that quality of being cut off from the rest of the world.

Out of Tama/Toledo on the fifth day, riders encountered ninety-five-degree heat and headwinds gusting up to thirty-five miles per hour. An estimated one-third of riders sagged that day, which went down in history as "Saggy Thursday."

Once again, RAGBRAI provided tons of local color. Webster City threw a renaissance fair, welcoming riders to "New Castle," the town's original name, and providing music, poetry, tumbling and jousting on bikes. Later that day, there were more people in Jolley (population forty-one) than any other day in its history. How did the town respond? With free neck rubs for riders. Down the road at Twin Lakes, cyclists were treated to free jet-ski rides.

1996–1997

In 1996, the overnight towns were the smallest ever, including Fayette with 910 permanent residents (given that Upper Iowa University was on summer vacation). This "little town that could" still managed to pull off a big welcome. Meanwhile, all nine residents of Seneca turned out to cheer RAGBRAI as it rode by.

In that crowd of cyclists was Team Aim High Air Force, with 130 cyclists. Another large group was composed of 300 cyclists taking part in the summer-long "Iowa 150 Bike Ride/A Sesquicentennial Expedition," part of Iowa's 150th anniversary. Offenburger led the group from Long Beach, California, on Memorial Day, through Iowa and on to Washington, D.C., on Labor Day. In its honor, RAGBRAI added seventy-eight miles to a seventy-two-mile day to create an optional 150-mile loop, which 1,100 riders completed.

On day three, Mr. Pork Chop, Paul Bernhard, challenged actor/comedian Tom Arnold to a contest hog calling "Pork Chooooop." When Bernard called him a "wimp," Arnold replied, "Hey, I was married to Rosanne for five years, so I don't think you can call me a wimp." Arnold was riding with a group of high school friends from his hometown of Ottumwa.

The University of Okoboji issued a press release that classes would be cancelled in honor of RAGBRAI. The only problem is that such a school does not exist. Another spoof occurred this year as Brian Mossman pedaled a stationary bike in the middle of a street in Milford while RAGBRAI cycled by.

The year 1997 started off looking scary when the route was announced: seven miles of gravel and twenty-five thousand feet uphill, the kind of climbing that is usually associated with cycling in the Rocky Mountains. "Hateful," is how Ann Karras described the route. In his defense, John Karras said that the main goals of this route were to include Des Moines and get the ride into Lucas County, the only one of Iowa's ninety-nine counties that RAGBRAI had not yet visited.

Despite all the climbing, the ride attracted the usual number of riders, drawn, perhaps, by the allure of the big city of Des Moines or the novelty of biking through tiny New York (population five), Bethlehem (population unknown) and Paris (population thirty) on the same day! Those must have been popular stops for holders of a souvenir passport issued by the U.S. Postal Service, a sponsor this year. Riders got special passport stamps at post offices along the route—even though that meant waiting in more lines (in addition to the many lines for food, showers, kybos, etc.).

The first day presented a problem worse than the many hills: thousands of thumbtacks spewed across the road, the second time such a stunt happened on RAGBRAI. Dozens of riders got flats, and one pulled nine tacks out of his tires.

When temperatures soar, cyclists have to work hard to stay hydrated.

About twenty-two thousand people participated in the festivities in Des Moines, which occurred at the Blank Park Zoo and old Fort Des Moines, well away from downtown. One hopes they made the most of it, as this would be the last time RAGBRAI stopped in the Capital City until 2013, sixteen years later.

For the first time, RAGBRAI visited Indianola, Pickard's hometown. The RAGBRAI pioneer's bike was on display, and his son, seventy-three-year-old Clarence "Jack" Pickard Jr., visited with cyclists. Indianola's hot air balloon races were scheduled to occur that week. On the day RAGBRAI rolled through town, the balloons were grounded due to fog and rain—yet there was no stopping the cyclists.

Another first was riding through the area made famous by the book and movie *Bridges of Madison County*.

1998

RAGBRAI surprised everyone with the announcement that Sabula would be the endpoint. Not only is Sabula tiny, with a population of 714—the smallest endpoint or overnight town ever—but also it's an island. How would the cyclists get there? Would all the cars, buses and trucks create gridlock? Would the island sink from the weight of RAGBRAI Nation?

Storm and tornado warnings disrupted RAGBRAI campers' sleep Saturday night, even before they had pedaled one mile. A free concert by the Cherokee Symphony Orchestra might have helped them sleep better on Sunday night. The concert was well received, in part because the conductor and several musicians were RAGBRAI cyclists.

Tom Vilsack, a Democratic candidate for governor, rode this year. "I kid you not," he said on his first day. "I biked more miles today than I have in my whole life." Despite this egregious lack of cycling experience, Vilsack went on to become governor of Iowa and agriculture secretary under President Barack Obama.

The route took riders through Jones County, home of Grant Wood, Iowa's most famous artist. Monticello (population 3,700) was full of visitors—12,000 for RAGBRAI *plus* 30,000 for the county fair. Food? Housing? Traffic? When Karla Decker, director of the Chamber of Commerce, was asked how things were going, she replied, "Not bad, but sometimes you just want to go 'Aaaaaaah.'"

Offenburger left the *Register* this year. In the meantime, another veteran RAGBRAIer, Carl Voss, took over for Mark Hilton as official pie judge. A self-proclaimed third-generation pie lover, Voss had been a pie judge at the Iowa State Fair, that other huge, iconic annual event in the Hawkeye state. This year, he gave the top RAGBRAI award to Martha Norman for her butterscotch meringue pie.

RAGBRAI XXVI had a few glitches. The main campground in Boone was left a mess. Traffic got considerably backed up at the end, where some participants reached Sabula over bridges and others were ferried across the Mississippi River to Savanna, Illinois, which shared closing duties with Sabula. But the good news was that the tiny island city didn't sink.

1999–2000

A few days before the ride began, a flood of the Cedar Rapids River ravaged the overnight town of Waverly, soaking sixty-five city blocks. It was uncertain whether the town would be able to host, as planned. "Everyone decided that no matter what, they were going to be ready," Tara Harn, executive director of the Waverly Chamber–Main

Street, told the *Register*. Volunteers moved sandbags, pumped water, raked mud and picked up debris. The fairground was a mess, but residents cleaned it up. The beer garden tent had collapsed, but they reassembled it. "Knowing that RAGBRAI was coming energized the whole town to recover more quickly from the flood than it would have otherwise," said Reverend Michael Burk of St. Paul's Lutheran Church.

Every year, cyclists struggling under Iowa's hot Iowa sun speculate (or boast) that they're enduring the hottest RAGBRAI ever. That was probably true in 1999. Temperatures hit the high nineties the first five days and 101 in Decorah the following day. High humidity drove the heat index up to 120 degrees, even as late as 10:00 p.m., making sleep all but impossible. How hot was it? Apparently even too hot for beer. Decorah's beer garden opened at 3:00 p.m. but had almost no patrons until six hours later. Also that day, patching materials on the road turned into liquid, splattering riders and bikes as they cycled through it. Many waited hours in the heat for a sag wagon. Probably not sagging, however, was sixty-five-year-old Edward Gelles riding his eighteenth RAGBRAI in a row on a 1941, single-speed Schwinn. He left his geared bikes at home as a point of pride and wore a T-shirt that says, "Gears R 4 wimps."

Those who quit early missed the *Register*'s 150th birthday party. In 1849, Gardner Cowles and Harvey Ingham of Algona moved to Des Moines and bought the newspaper that became the *Register*, so in 1999 the paper celebrated in Algona with ten thousand cupcakes. Another festival, of sorts, debuted this year: RAGBRAI's Expo of vendors, bike shops and others.

Brian Duffy's cartoon reveals the truth about RAGBRAI. As Donald Kaul put it, "I hurt all over, top to bottom, inside and out. If I gave my body to science, science would give it back." *From the* Des Moines Register. *Reprinted with permission.*

Karras retired as co-host in 2000, saying he'd rather participate as a rider than work the event. Brian Duffy, the *Register*'s political cartoonist, stepped up. He was an avid cyclist and loved RAGBRAI. Soon, like Karras, he wished he could ride it rather than work it. "I started getting envious of all those people sitting in the beer gardens, while I still had work to do," Duffy says. "The good thing was that there was always lots going on to inspire cartoons."

Even after twenty-eight years, RAGBRAI continued to produce surprises. The Iowa Department for Public Health set up weigh stations for cyclists at the start and finish. Of the 125 cyclists who weighed themselves before and after, the men lost nearly two pounds on average and the women gained a little more than a pound.

Still, everything didn't work smoothly. This year, Burlington was slow getting ready to host. "There seems to be some feet-dragging and a lackadaisical attitude," Richard Luckenbill, a local cyclist told the *Register*. "Things should've been done in February that weren't done until May."

RAGBRAI organizers in Burlington acknowledged that several committee members had quit but dismissed claims that they were short of help or didn't want the ride. "Ending towns always get the short end of RAGBRAI," Luckenbill said, because they make only a fraction of the money other towns get from food stands and beer gardens. "(Riders) come in, dip their tires and leave. People here are saying, 'Why should we do all this planning when we won't reap the benefits?'"

2001–2002

Highlights of 2001 included an overnight in Coralville, where students from Kate Wickham Elementary School had conducted a postcard-writing campaign a year earlier to entice RAGBRAI to come to their town. Also, the ride passed what was then billed as the world's largest wind farm, where about 280 wind turbines dotted the eighteen-mile stretch between Storm Lake and Alta. Each one stood two hundred feet tall, with blades seventy-six feet long. And an overnight in Grinnell highlighted its impressive architecture: Victorian and Prairie School homes, a lovely college campus, Louis Sullivan's 1914 "Jewel Box Bank" and an Andrew Carnegie library.

Riders might have noticed the changing face of Iowa, with a small but growing Latino population. Hispanics make up the state's largest minority group, as evidenced by the increasing number of Hispanic food vendors along RAGBRAI, especially in three 2001 overnight towns that happen to have some of the largest percentages of Hispanics in Iowa: Denison (17 percent), Storm Lake (20 percent) and Perry (25 percent).

RAGBRAI

Starting with this year, the optional loop was named the John Karras Loop.

The opening ceremonies for 2002 in Sioux Center were in remembrance of the tragedies that had occurred on September 11, 2001. Especially poignant was the presence of Team Escape made up primarily of policemen and firefighters from New York City, some of whom had been personally impacted by the World Trade Center bombing. On Wednesday, Remembrance Day, many riders wore patriotic attire, and military planes flew overhead.

With the increased use of MP3 players and iPods, RAGBRAI participants created playlists that helped keep them pedaling across Iowa. All seemed to feature Bicycle Race, by Queen, while the ultimate RAGBRAI playlist, at least for a Boomer, included: "On the Road Again" (Willie Nelson); "Watching the Wheels" (John Lennon); "Rockin' Down the Highway" (the Doobie Brothers); "Wrong Road Again" (Crystal Gayle); and "Born to Run" (Bruce Springsteen). Depending on the weather, these songs would

This photograph was shot in 2010, but similar patriotic displays were common on RAGBRAI XXX in remembrance of September 11, 2001. *Ken Urban Photography.*

also be appropriate: "Against the Wind" (Bob Seger); "Riders on the Storm" (the Doors); "Ring of Fire" (Johnny Cash); and "Stayin' Alive" (the Bee Gees).

Still, many cyclists blasted their music preferences for all to hear, often with a simple boom box, sometimes with a sizeable sound system pulled on a trailer. I'm glad I did not ride a year when the "Macarena" was popular.

It rained so hard on the last night of the ride that tractors were needed to pull buses and trucks out of the mud in Bellevue.

2003–2004

For the first time, the route stayed in the southern, hillier portion of the state for the entire week. This meant more than twenty-three thousand feet of climbing, one of the highest ever. Riders may not have appreciated the hills, but a number of struggling towns and counties appreciated the economic boost and morale lift that RAGBRAI brought right to their doorsteps, especially the eleven towns that had never been visited before. Many of these southern Iowa communities were struggling due to recent job and population losses.

Greg LeMond, the first American to win the Tour de France (1986, 1989 and 1990), rode part of the ride and visited with admirers. He attracted large crowds, but not nearly as large as Lance Armstrong would when he participated starting in 2006.

This year saw renewed efforts to enforce liquor laws, some of which had been ignored in recent years. In 2001, the Iowa Alcoholic Beverages Division abandoned an effort to monitor RAGBRAI due to budget cuts, and the Iowa State Patrol stepped in to fill the void. This year, troopers met with liquor-license holders about the need to observe laws, such as those prohibiting the serving of minors. They also advised the beer gardens and local bars not to allow customers to leave their premises with open drinks.

In 2003, Green announced he would retire. After T.J. Juskiewicz was selected as the next director, Green agreed to stay another year to help him transition into the job. Together, they faced a tough year in 2004. On the first day, three cyclists fell within one hundred yards of one another due to catching their front tires in an inch-wide crack in the centerline seam of a road in Crawford County. One of them, Kirk Ullrich, died, which sparked a controversy surrounding the rights and responsibilities of riders and the liabilities and responsibilities of counties (see the chapter "Shift Happens"). This accident was RAGBRAI's first fatality from a bike crash with no other factors involved.

Things Green addressed during his tenure were underage drinking and excessive partying. "I didn't want RAGBRAI to be known as the biggest party in the world, so I took steps to curb reckless behavior," he says. "We had to work, even negotiate, with many of the rowdy teams to get them to play by the rules."

Iowa is surprisingly hilly. *Photo by Bob Frank, PBV.*

After a bike ride in Georgia had an E. coli breakout, Green increased Health Department inspections of food vendors. He also improved working relations with host communities and got local committees more involved in planning and execution.

"One of the things I'm proudest of was getting communities to work together," Green says. "People in some of these towns have a lot of territoriality. They don't want to give up anything. And the churches have their own agendas. But through RAGBRAI, they learned that they could accomplish more working together as a team."

Chapter 6

A FAMILY AFFAIR

The Juskiewicz Years

In 1996, Juskiewicz was working for the Florida Governor's Council on Fitness and Health when he heard RAGBRAI coordinator Jim Green give a presentation about the Iowa ride during a national business meeting. Already developing a big bike ride in Florida, Juskiewicz was intrigued with RAGBRAI's story. He finally got around to riding it in 2002 and was impressed with its size, scope and organization.

"I never envisioned myself living in Iowa, but Green told me he was going to retire and encouraged me to apply for the job, which I got," Juskiewicz says. "Convincing my wife to give up Florida for Iowa was the toughest part, but neither of us has any regrets."

One of Juskiewicz's key goals has been to preserve the ride and its traditions. "Every RAGBRAI is different, but the philosophy of how we go about working with the towns will remain the same," he told the *Register* shortly after he was named assistant director under Green.

Ten years later, that was still true. "The Expo and some of the entertainment are bigger, but once you get on your bike, the experience is very similar to what it was ten, twenty years ago," he says. "You don't see McDonald's or Starbucks along the way. It's still Iowa hospitality that makes things work."

Another goal of his has been to make the ride more family friendly. Indeed, more families and extended families have been participating. Thus, while baby-boomers on RAGBRAI are reliving their youth, second- and third-generation riders are *living* theirs.

Juskiewicz never seems to get tired of talking about RAGBRAI. Once while on vacation at Disney World, a man named Randy Bunkers noticed his Iowa T-shirt and asked him what he did for a living. When Juskiewicz said he was the director of RAGBRAI, Bunkers said, "I run a doughnut shop in Jefferson, Iowa, where I'm on the city council, and I hereby invite RAGBRAI to pass through Jefferson," Juskiewicz says. RAGBRAI obliged the following year, and Juskiewicz always stops at Bunkers Dunkers when he visits Jefferson.

Top: Go Hawks! *Ken Urban Photography.*

Bottom: This family of four looks sharp. T.J. Juskiewicz has tried to make RAGBRAI more family friendly. *Photo by Bob Frank.*

2005

Tragedy struck a month before the ride started. Ultra-marathon cyclist Breedlove died when his bike collided head-on with a pickup truck in Colorado during the Race Across America. Breedlove was an inspiration to other RAGBRAIers, who will remember him for his favorite saying, "Another day in paradise." He was honored at a ceremony in Norwood in the middle of RAGBRAI XXXIII.

Another tragedy occurred this year. During the second night, heavy rains and winds gusting as strong as seventy miles per hour ravaged campsites. In a freak accident, the storm blew a tree limb twenty inches in diameter onto Michael Burke's tent, apparently killing him instantly.

This year served up RAGBRAI's usual fare of fun and games. In Le Mars, the self-declared First Ice Cream Capital of the World and home of Blue Bunny Ice Cream, handed out twenty-five thousand ice cream treats. Towns toward the end of the ride always have to work harder to attract and impress their visitors, but resourceful towns at the end of this week offered polka classes, the chance to pet a camel and a frozen T-shirt contest. Yes, a farmer in Spillville froze T-shirts with liquid nitrogen that he uses for animal breeding. To win a prize, the contestant had to be the first to break open and don the hard T-shirt.

2006–2007

Lance Armstrong thrilled RAGBRAI by riding a couple of days in 2006. His presence was nothing short of electrifying. Kenneth "King Kenny" Groezinger, a twenty-six-year RAGBRAI veteran, spotted Armstrong three times this week and was giddy about shaking his hand. Steve Isaacson, a member of C.U.B.S. who had ridden fifteen RAGBRAIs, told the *Register* in 2011, "I've probably spent 650 hours riding RAGBRAI, and the most exciting three seconds was watching Lance fly by."

Armstrong addressed a huge, adoring crowd of twenty thousand in Newton, exhorting them to use Iowa's powerful influence in selecting the next U.S. president to demand more funding for cancer research. He would return to RAGBRAI in 2007, 2008 and 2011.

Meanwhile, there was "trouble in the State of Iowa." In response to the lawsuit concerning Ullrich's death, Crawford County banned RAGBRAI to avoid liability.

2008–2009

Crawford County's ban did not last long. When it rescinded the ban in 2008, RAGBRAI was, once again, cleared for takeoff statewide.

Jefferson hosted a retirement party for Paul Bernhard, Mr. Pork Chop, but his family was planning to continue the pork chop and pink bus tradition, even if they couldn't match his famous "pork choooop" call.

With the bombastic rock band Styx performing in 2008, old-timers complained that RAGBRAI had become too big, glitzy and commercialized. By this time, RAGBRAI had about twenty sponsors, known as Friends of RAGBRAI. This included the likes of Google and Best Western, as well as Iowa Economic Development.

Matt "Mr. Pork Chop Jr." Bernhard has taken over the grill in the family business, started by Paul Bernhard in 1983.

At the same time, the bike ride itself maintained its local charm. The ride passed through three of the Amana Colonies, one of Iowa's more colorful, historic and enduring communities. And picturesque Le Claire, the last town in 2008, is known for an annual Tugfest tug-of-war with Port Byron, Illinois, which stretches a rope across the Mississippi, something that is rarely allowed because it shuts down river traffic.

There were plenty of cool things to see the following year, including fainting goats in Mineola (it's a defense mechanism); a nighttime hot air balloon show in Indianola; and Stanton's water towers, which are decorated like a coffee pot and tea cup. Every house in Stanton used to be white until a nonconformist painted one blue in 2009. And Sandyville (population sixty) got its first traffic light, but only for a day. The light was affixed to a beer tent that was dismantled that night.

2010—2012

RAGBRAI was, indeed, getting bigger and more commercialized, as evidenced by the festivities in Sioux City, headlined by Smash Mouth and attended by an estimated twenty-five thousand people. The Expo was bigger than ever, and Spin Doctors performed on Tuesday night. This trend toward big-name entertainment continued with such bands as Grand Funk Railroad in 2011 and Three Dog Night and Counting Crows in 2012.

Bob Dorr, leader of the Blue Band, which has played RAGBRAI about twenty-five times, says he laments the fact that RAGBRAI encourages overnight towns to hire nationally known performers. "Anymore, I prefer to play during the day, when shows are not so big and entertainment can be more relaxed and spontaneous," he says.

Juskiewicz says RAGBRAI still hires mostly local bands but adds, "RAGBRAI is not just for the riders. Local residents, who have volunteered thousands of hours, want to celebrate, too. For them, RAGBRAI lasts one day, and they like the big names."

While it's hard to outshine decades of RAGBRAI entertainment and activities, Manning came up with one of the most impressive RAGBRAI projects ever: a huge corn maze spread over three acres that riders were invited to explore. When seen from the air, the beautifully rendered maze depicted RAGBRAI's logo and the 2011 route across a 1,365-foot-long outline of Iowa. The town of 1,490 people gave out as many postcards featuring an aerial view of the maze.

Riders keep amazing others, too, year after year. One of the two men pictured on the cover of the 2012 Participant Guide was Scott Mills, who had been diagnosed with non-Hodgkin's lymphoma in May. The forty-one-year-old man had to take two days off RAGBRAI XL for chemotherapy, but he still finished the ride.

Despite its age, RAGBRAI XL found more towns to visit for the first time. Alleman and White Oak had never hosted RAGBRAI, and Altoona had never been an

Profile of RAGBRAI XL riders 2012	
Gender	32% women; 68% men
Age	44.5 years, average age
Experience	33% rode RAGBRAI for first time
Teams	4,000 (many with two members)
Income	69% over $75,000 (per household)
Occupation	80% professional or management
Education	90% of adults are college graduates
From Iowa	37% Iowa residents
Origin	All 50 states; 18 foreign countries
Source: RAGBRAI	

Bikes take
a rest after
untold mi…
Photo by B…
Frank.

overnight town. And *due* to its age, RAGBRAI was becoming tamer, or "lamer," as rider Mitch Daniels put it. "I still look forward to getting up and riding every day, but it's not like it used to be," he told the *Register*. "RAGBRAI is politically correct now." On the other hand, some say that the raucous behavior continues at the back of the pack and off the route.

Still, RAGBRAI has a small-town, *Leave It to Beaver* quality. In Story City, riders got off their bikes and took a different kind of spin—a ride on a ninety-nine-year-old carousel. Zearing held goldfish races in roof gutters. And Clemons offered an unusual dunk tank. The victim would sit on a bench under a platform holding a toilet, and when the ball hit a big red target, the toilet would splash the victim with water.

RAGBRAI's 2012 fortieth-anniversary bash in Cedar Rapids honored seven cyclists who had participated every year: Randy Dickson, Scott Dickson, James Hopkins, Nancy Jo Hopkins, Carter LeBeau, Margaret Paulos and Rick Paulos.

Chapter 7

TEAMS

The Good, the Bad, the Ugly

R AGBRAI teams provide much of the color, character and, yes, mischief found on RAGBRAI—or anywhere on two wheels.

An increasing number of RAGBRAIers ride with a team (or a charter, which performs many of the same functions). By 2003, there were 950 registered teams of five or more riders. For most cyclists, the team they choose goes a long way toward defining their experience during the week. Team Ronald McDonald House Charities Iowa will offer a different look and feel, pace and schedule, than Team Blazing Saddles.

On a practical level, most teams transport riders to the starting town; carry their luggage; provide some food, beverages and entertainment; and then transport riders back to or near their hometown. Some teams may offer a variety of comforts and services such as showers, recharging stations and tent set up. Team leaders help handle registration, find housing or a campsite and sometimes provide a team gift.

More important than logistics, teams generate spirit and provide riders with social activities, a culture and even an identity. Many have creative names and distinctive costumes, such as Team Tutu, whose motto is "You can never have tutu much fun." Others have amusing traditions, droll rites and decorated, customized vans or buses that serve as headquarters.

These colorful, sometimes wacky buses typically come with a bike rack, rooftop patio and music system. Some provide couches and sleeping accommodations. One had a putting green on its roof. In most cases, these rolling clubhouses seem to shout "paaarty." Passengers have been known to play loud music, drink a lot, moon passing vehicles and engage in other shenanigans. The online Museum of RAGBRAI Buses (http://morb1.tripod.com) describes and depicts thirty-six outlandish buses, complete with their Latin names. Team Generic's bus, *Plainus Machinus,* "resembles the minimalist art of the 1950s, taking the everyday object and degrading it to its lowest form with a hint of bold commercialism."

Team buses present an eye- and ear-full and serve as team clubhouses. *From the* Des Moines Register. *Reprinted with permission.*

Some team names are quite literal. Team Grinnell is made up of alum from a liberal arts college in, well, Grinnell, while the Des Moines Cycle Club is, in a sense, the hometown team. Then there's Team Wedgie and Team Waldo. Spin Docs was a team of six doctors, but you may have to think about Team Megasaurus for a second. (What gets sore after biking a long time?) One hopes that Team Fungus Amongus ("We grow on you") doesn't belong in this literal category. Meanwhile, Team Crank Addicts could describe everyone on RAGBRAI.

Other team names aim to shock, such as Team Kybo and Team Road Kill, which decorates dead animals along the road with beads and stickers. Team Me Off invites each member to personalize his or her name by filling in the blank, as in Flip Me Off, Piss Me Off or worse. Team Killer Bees allows for similar individualism. Members include "May Bee," "Wanna Bee," "Bee Ware" and, my favorite, "Bee Zerk."

Some teams stand out more than others. Riding in 1993, Team Malibu was composed of six twelve-year-old boys (Little League teammates from Southern California) with their moms. That same year, Team Wimpy Dave created a stir. For months, Dave Rix had planned to ride RAGBRAI with his sister and brother-in-law. After Dave backed out, they went without him, wearing T-shirts saying, "Team Wimpy Dave." His sister and brother-in-law also handed out stamped, preaddressed postcards, asking fellow riders to write to Dave about what a great time they were having. Plus, they talked to *Register* columnist Chuck Offenburger, who chided Dave in the paper. After receiving dozens of postcards and reading about himself in the paper, Dave caved. He grabbed a bike and joined the ride for the last day, wearing a T-shirt saying, "I'm wimpy Dave," for which he caught much flak.

Many teams sport costumes that riff off their names. Team Dairy Air wears cowbells while Team Dragbrai's outfit is self-explanatory. Team Pie Hunters wears Styrofoam slices of different flavors of pie on their helmets. Team Flamingo wears pink feather boas attached to their helmets, while Team Spin sports wild purple wigs. It's not known what Team Naked wears.

Other teams have cute mottos. Team Cow: "Playing well with udders since 2004." Team Dawg: "Known to shake some tail." Team Plywood: "Easy to lay, fun to nail." And Team Three Sheets claims that its name refers to a love of sailing.

Having "cycled down," Team Spin takes a break. RAGBRAI provides great people-watching for riders and residents. *Janet Kersey Kowal.*

RAGBRAI

Some team names need explaining. Women of N.I.P.S: "Not in perfect shape." Carl Voss likes to tease people about his team. When asked if he rides with a team, he replies, "Not Exactly." Pause. Yes, that's the name of his team, which has been riding together since 1991. "There's plenty that we're 'not exactly,'" Voss adds.

Notorious for partying, self-contained Team Bad Boy has been known to haul its own lawn chairs, cooler, grill and well-stocked, foldout bar. One year they brought along the kitchen sink, complete with running water—or was that beer? Their luxury gear and accouterments weigh up to eighty-five pounds per rider, and the Bad Boys take pride in being among the last to arrive in each overnight town.

Counterbalancing the rowdy and risqué teams are serious ones. There have been many rolling Alcoholics Anonymous chapters. In 1999, the Iowa Department of Natural Resources organized a team that took turns riding a homemade solar-assisted bicycle. And Pedaling for Parkinson's has monitored the performance of some of its members to determine the effects of biking on their symptoms. "I was told to give up cycling because Parkinson's was taking away my ability to balance," said Jim Wetherell, a team member in 2006. "But I decided to add one wheel rather than selling two. I bought a recumbent tricycle. That was five years and more than thirty thousand miles ago!"

Someone on a unicycle is likely to be a member of Team Roadshow, a group of jugglers, clowns, musicians and acrobats who finance their way across the state by performing. These "rapscallions" have been entertaining riders since 2003 "with pranks and tomfoolery," says one member.

One of the most inspirational teams is the Dream Team, brainchild of former RAGBRAI coordinator Jim Green. Free of charge, it's open to Des Moines teenagers who are financially disadvantaged or have behavioral problems. Some of the kids have never been outside of Des Moines. RAGBRAI, Bike World and the Riverfront YMCA founded the team in 1997. The training starts indoors at the YMCA in the cold of January, and the reward comes at the Mississippi River in the heat of July. Experienced volunteer cyclists coach the kids through their training and chaperone them across the state. If the members finish, they get to keep the bike and equipment they used to train and ride.

Chris Crane, eighteen, who would become a senior at East High School in the fall of 2001, was on his second RAGBRAI with the Dream Team. "I like things that take energy," he told the *Register*. "Cycling is pretty fun, and this is a nice workout." Frank Long, one of the Dream Team's adult volunteers, said, "What I want the kids to take away from this is skill building, teamwork, self-esteem, confidence and learning that they can accomplish something."

In 2012, more than four thousand teams participated, most of them informal groups of two or more family or friends without a team name or jersey. Such was the case with Mark Wyatt, executive director of the Iowa Bicycle Coalition, who rode with eight friends. "We didn't start early; we just tried to have fun on the ride," Wyatt says. "Stopping can be as much fun as going.

"Each of us gets only one 'melt-down' ticket per week," he adds, "so if you use it on Sunday or Monday you have to be good the rest of the week!"

FIRST TEAM

During the first two RAGBRAIs, there were no teams. Little by little, however, riders formed teams and gave themselves names. In some cases, preexisting bike clubs fielded RAGBRAI teams, but the most creative teams grew out of RAGBRAI itself. Some have come and gone (not to be confused with Team Kum & Go, composed of co-workers and friends from a convenience-store chain); others have persevered for more than thirty years.

Old-timers will debate what constitutes a "team" and which one was the first. Team Kobberdahl formed in 1975, which, "in my book," makes it the oldest team to

Members of the Kobberdahl clan—RAGBRAI's first team—in their homemade "uniforms" on RAGBRAI III in Hawarden. *Steve Kobberdahl.*

organize around RAGBRAI. Steve Kobberdahl recounts that his father rode RAGBRAI II and liked it so much that he bought his three sons (ages nine, eleven and thirteen) ten-speeds for Christmas, when he announced that they would ride RAGBRAI together the following year. Steve's stepmother made bike jerseys (a novelty in Iowa at that time) for the four Kobberdahls and six friends by sewing a RAGBRAI patch on the front of each T-shirt and pockets on the back. "How she knew way back then in Iowa that a bike jersey had pockets I'll never know, but we thought they were pretty cool," Steve says.

The team rode together for five years, sleeping in a large canvas tent. "Our family did a lot to spread the word early on about what a great ride this is," says Steve, who has more than thirty RAGBRAIs under his belt. Judging from Steve's stories, Karras and Kaul knew the Kobberdahls and appreciated their enthusiastic support. In 1987, Karras wrote about Steve's brother Doug, who had ridden twelve RAGBRAIs before dying of leukemia at the age of twenty-five. Karras recognized that Kobberdahl family and friends would be calling the ride that year "DOUGBRAI" in recognition of Doug's indomitable spirit. "If you see shirts with 'DOUGBRAI' on them," he wrote in the paper, "tip your hat in acknowledgement of a fallen comrade."

Oldest Team Still Around

Most people in the know recognize Team Skunk as the first official team founded for RAGBRAI that has survived to this day. It's certainly one of the proudest, counting among its members cycling icon Greg LeMond; Ben Cohen of Ben and Jerry's Ice Cream; and Ben Davidson, an Oakland Raiders star. Founder Tim Lane likes to include everyone who has ever ridden with the team as a member for life. By that count, Team Skunk has more than 500 members, although it currently fields a team of about 120.

Lane calls the team "a carpool that got way outta hand." It grew out of a decision to carpool to RAGBRAI taken by him and Ann Vorwald after a softball game in Ames along the Skunk River, thus the name.

When the team's first uniform, a black T-shirt with a large white stripe down the back, proved to be too hot, most Skunks switched to bike jerseys. Still, members are encouraged to wear black and white every day. The heat does not stop them from wearing tuxedoes, ties and cummerbunds for their annual "formal day" during the ride.

Team Skunk includes among its many accomplishments helping to develop and promote the Ride Right safety campaign. It also helped "save" RAGBRAI in Elkader in 1980 when cyclists and locals got dangerously rowdy in response to a derisive article about RAGBRAI (see the chapter "Shift Happens"). "When we saw that things were getting unruly, Skunks asked bar owners to turn down the music, got garbage bags and picked up trash and helped move the 'party' out of the main street onto a side street," Lane says.

Team Skunk is old school. It has kept its costs down to $160 for 2013 (not including the *Register*'s $150 fee). And it does not have a team bus because it's more focused on biking rather than just going along for the ride, says Patti Campidilli, who has helped run the team since joining in 1983. "Some teams use the bus to party, but we strive to bike every mile." Bearing that out, some of RAGBRAI's most ardent cyclists have been members, including Frank "Huck" Thompson, who rode every mile for the first thirty-five years, and Karras, who rode with Team Skunk for six or seven years after retiring.

Helping to run the team is a lot of work, but a desire to encourage people to challenge themselves keeps Campidilli engaged. "It's good for people to push themselves, and this is one of the best, safest ways for them to do that," she says.

FAR FROM HOME

One of the teams that has come the farthest to ride RAGBRAI is Team Venito starting in 1999 and continuing for several years. A region in Italy, Venito is paired with Iowa as an international sister state. Italy is crazy about biking, and members of Team Venito were extremely talented cyclists.

They were a far cry from the nasty, vain Italian cyclists portrayed in *Breaking Away*, the most popular bicycle movie ever made. Like the Italians in the film, however, they do ride fast. During its first year, Team Venito completed most of the daily distances in three hours or less. "Slow down! It isn't a race," Amy Worthen, a volunteer with Iowa Sister State, implored them. They did, but only a little.

"They were very fast, almost at a professional level," says Jim Leonardo of Des Moines, who rode with the team one year. Leonardo was a lifelong cyclist who had biked from Des Moines to Central America. Nevertheless, he couldn't keep up with Team Venito. "The only ones who could were members of Team Air Force, and they enjoyed racing each other," Leonardo says.

Team Venito certainly dressed well. "They don't have the ratty casualness that most of the other RAGBRAI riders do," Worthen told the *Register* in 2000. "Their style is as important as their riding, and their bikes are ultra-bright, ultra-lightweight and ultra-expensive."

TEAM GOURMET

Scarfing down a pork chop wrapped in a paper towel while waiting in line for pie, or eating an ear of corn-on-the-cob while the melted margarine runs down your arm, is part of RAGBRAI's charm. In the evening, however, some prefer using a fork and knife to eat a carefully prepared meal off a plate while chatting with friends and sipping a glass of wine—aka dining. For them there's Team Gourmet, which takes members on a culinary crusade across Iowa every July.

This Chicago-based team of foodies travels with its own chefs and fridges and freezers full of fine food. Every night, the chefs put on a sit-down banquet at the home of a local host, many of whom vie for the pleasure and bragging rights of hosting this iconic team.

Team Gourmet, which has been featured in *Midwest Living*, *Saveur* and *Gourmet* magazines and on *Iron Chef America*, prints its weeklong menu on its team jersey. That makes each member a walking, talking, biking tribute to the team's epicurean experience. When a fellow RAGBRAIer spots a Team Gourmeter, the typical greeting is, "Hey, what's for dinner?" That could be anything from lobster bisque followed by garlic-sautéed frog legs to potato pancake bilini with caviar and iced vodka shots followed by portobello polenta.

When amateur chef Wayne Santi and his friends and family started Team Gourmet in 1996, they cooked and camped outside. Now the team cooks in hosts' kitchens and sleeps inside.

Wayne Santi and his family and friends started Team Gourmet in 1996 after they had ridden RAGBRAI for a few years. One day, a friend dropped out of their group, saying he was tired of searching for a good dinner every night. "The sauce is burnt at the church basement while over at the school cafeteria they're out of everything except potatoes and carrots," he told Dana Santi, Wayne's daughter.

The solution: amateur chef Wayne would cook. He quickly realized, however, that cooking and cycling was tougher than he thought, primarily because the group camped out. Wayne would bike half the day, cook outdoors and then wash up with a hose. It was so tough that he had a RAGBRAI heart attack. After that scare, Wayne stopped biking but kept cooking for the team. The work became easier after he took on an assistant and the team started staying in homes, where the chefs could work from a kitchen and everyone slept indoors.

Membership on Team Gourmet was limited to family and friends, but it grew to more than fifty bon vivants. This proved to be unmanageable, given the group's ambitious gastronomic goals. In addition, some members didn't agree with the

Peter DeLucci and Paul Naughton enjoy a stop along RAGBRAI's border-to-border buffet line in 2010. *Janet Kersey Kowal.*

rising price to participate, brought about, in part, by purchasing cooking gear and equipment. "We tried to get everyone to pay dues to support the team because we were getting tired of borrowing this aunt's freezer and that high school's grill," Dana explains.

In 2004, the team split in two with the spin-off calling itself Team Cuisine, running on a tighter budget and camping out rather than staying in homes. Janet Kersey Kowal and Tim Hart took over management of Team Gourmet in 2010 after the Santis couldn't continue.

For 2013, it cost $820 to ride and eat with Team Gourmet. That does not include RAGBRAI's $150 fee but just about everything else: jersey, T-shirt, nightly meals, transportation, inside sleeping accommodations, team dues and team donations to nonprofits.

Every night, before sitting down to dine at tables spread out over their host's yard or driveway, each team member introduces himself or herself to the hosts, who join the team for dinner. The idea is to get to know the hosts rather than just bunking in their house. "We love the interaction and the friendships that grow out of this," Kersey Kowal says. "I like to tell our hosts that we're easier to have than relatives."

When Kersey Kowal turned forty, she asked herself what she really loves to do, and RAGBRAI came in at the top of her list. Ever since, she's devoted much of her free time to the team and the ride.

Having ridden her first RAGBRAI in 1979 with Team Kobberdahl, Kersey Kowal is well known in RAGBRAI circles and around the state. Her uncle was the mayor of Grand Junction. Another uncle and aunt have a farm outside Paton. And her dad was a banker who traveled all over the state, and she has met many of those contacts. "With me and RAGBRAI, it's only two degrees of separation," she says. "In fact, someone once asked me if I was related to all those people. 'Let's not go there!' I answered, with a laugh."

Team S.N.I.F.F.

Team S.N.I.F.F. is a frequent guest of Team Gourmet. Formed in 1988 by four buddies, it has built up a reputation for partying and irreverent behavior. Its motto is, "Meet in the first bar on the left…unless it's on the right."

Members refuse to divulge the meaning of their acronym, offering only the remote possibility that it might stand for "Some Nice Innocent Fine Fellows." Their reticence prompts many people to try to decipher the acronym, with many guesses unfit to print. When the team went co-ed several years ago, a name change was not required, indicating that the final "F" never stood for "Fellows."

Team S.N.I.F.F. is known for organizing entertaining drinking games. In one, the team gives complete strangers a loud cheer and standing ovation when they enter a bar. In the so-called Grape Game, team members draw a stick man on the ground in front of a bar and place grapes or olives where the figure's testicles would be. When a passerby happens to crush the grapes or olives, everyone cracks up.

Co-founder Ken "King Kenny" Groezinger claims the team introduced RAGBRAI to lick-on tattoos in 1993. "We had a blast that year." Some members took the next step by getting real tattoos, he adds. "We had 'Team S.NI.F.F.' tattooed on our right ankle so everyone could tell who was passing them!" To clear the way for their pace line, they would use an air horn and call out "car back."

The team is always looking for a laugh. A 1998 newsletter describes PRAGDS (Post RAG Depression Syndrome) as being "listless and apathetic about real life; waking before dawn thinking you hear the zip of nearby tents; craving adult beverages before the 'Today Show' signs on; ignoring watches and newspapers." To bring this scourge "out of the shadows into the light of day," the newsletter announced the formation of a PRAGDS support group, saying, "The first meeting will be held in a small Iowa town in the first bar on the left…unless it's on the right."

TALL DOG BIKE CLUB

Another longstanding team is the Tall Dog Bike Club. Its name comes from the name of a powerboat owned by a friend of Dwayne Barton's, one of the founders of the club. "We wanted to say, 'It takes a pretty tall dog to be in our club and do our activities,'" he explains.

In addition to enjoying a party and drinking their share of beer, such activities included dancing, water slides and, years ago, when the roads were less crowded, bike follies, with cyclists riding in formation, weaving in and out. Today, Tall Dog parties less but still has a good time.

The club motto is "A leg-up on the rest;" its campsite is called "The Dog Pound;" its newsletter prints "All the poop that's fit to print;" and its bike trailer is called "The Gallows." (Someone said the club's original trailer looked like a gallows, and the name stuck.) The original trailer carried about twenty bikes, but as the club grew, it needed a bigger trailer, and its members asked for more amenities. The third version of The Gallows, a twin-axle, flatbed trailer, carries more than fifty bikes and includes four flip-out showers, a tankless water heating system, lights and a phone recharging station.

Tall Dog accommodates about 125 riders and in 2012 charged $165 for the full week (not counting the *Register*'s $150 fee). "As a not-for-profit, we're not looking to make any money from this," says Steve "Eman" Engeman, who has ridden with the team for twenty-nine consecutive years, running it since 2000. He's the designer and builder of the trailer and other team contrivances. It shows that he owns and operates a building-design firm and comes from a construction background.

Other conveniences that Tall Dog has added in recent years include a tent concierge service, a one-hundred-cup coffee maker and a four-burner, flattop griddle that allows a cook to prepare breakfast for those willing to pay. "Who knows what's next, but I enjoy the hell out of doing this," Engeman says.

"Despite a few comforts, RAGBRAI still presents a physical challenge," he adds. "Five hundred miles of Iowa is still five hundred miles of Iowa."

Team awards set many tails wagging every year: Three-Legged Dog (for the most mechanical problems), Greyhound (fastest rider) and Best in Show (overall). The club is also known for its creative nicknames, says Julie Engeman, who has ridden twenty-five RAGBRAIs. One guy who rode his bike through a McDonald's drive-through window became known as "Drive Through." "Check Mark" got her name by looking at a T-shirt with lizards "doing it" in various positions and checking off the ones she had tried. Angel got nicknamed "Devil," and then there's "Mad Dog," "Corn Dog," etc.

"We're very close and kid around a lot," Julie says. In 2009, more than a dozen members dressed up as characters from *The Wizard of Oz*. They were inspired by the idea because RAGBRAI takes courage and heart…but not brains. In any case, the Tin Man's oilcan must have come in handy!

C.U.B.S.

C.U.B.S. stands for Chicago Urban Bicycling Society, and it's a championship team, despite its namesake. Former RAGBRAI coordinator Jim Green calls C.U.B.S. the Cadillac of teams. It was founded in 1996 by a group of riders who were not satisfied with the services of a company they had used on a few RAGBRAIs.

Former leader Jerry Turry has confirmed many times that a team's name is important because it projects an image. "Even though we don't represent a baseball team, it helps that Iowans like their Cubs [an affiliate of the Chicago Cubs], that the Chicago Cubs are so well known and that our name is easy to remember," Turry says.

It helped in 2000 when C.U.B.S. was competing with Team Dirty Rotten Bastards for permission to camp in the backyards of some homeowners in Waukee. (Guess who got the nod.) Still, a couple of times, the team has come close to sending a member home, such as the one who overserved himself and peed off a porch in front of the hosts.

With a large group of about sixty members, C.U.B.S. has had to be creative in finding accommodations. It pioneered the idea of staying in funeral homes, which are typically large and air-conditioned. That worked fine except for the time there

Residents of Sioux Center welcome C.U.B.S. in 2012. The team took up the backyards, dens and basements of four homes.

was a funeral when the C.U.B.S. were scheduled to stay. The team had to split up and scramble for other accommodations.

C.U.B.S. supports Camp Courageous, a large, privately funded camp in Monticello that helps disabled people of all ages. C.U.B.S. has raised more than $75,000 for the camp through donations, an auction during its annual banquet held during RAGBRAI and kybo roulette. In this game, people in line for a kybo are asked to bet which door will open next. C.U.B.S. biggest gift to Camp Courageous was the first train car for the small passenger railroad running through the facility's grounds.

C.U.B.S. has some strong cyclists. Dave McWhinnie, a Skokie, Illinois dentist, is such a strong rider that after he rolls into the overnight town he's been known to hitch up his powered paraglider and take off for the skies, even once after biking the grueling Karras Loop. While powered paragliders occasionally appear on RAGBRAI, it's rare that an individual has the energy to bike and pilot one.

McWhinnie became interested in powered paragliding and RAGBRAI more than ten years ago when he and his wife, Minda, became empty-nesters. "I like the independence of both these sports and the way they take me close to nature," he says. "Each one offers almost a religious experience…to be really immersed in the natural world."

The skies over RAGBRAI have seen powered paragliders and hot air balloons, biplanes and fighter planes. *Photo by Dave McWhinnie.*

C.U.B.S. has been home to Mike Conklin, a former *Chicago Tribune* reporter and team chronicler. He likes to tell the story of the night the team camped in the backyard of a large home in Iowa City where the owner forgot to mention that the grounds were equipped with an automatic sprinkler system. "We were all awakened at two or three in the morning, as campers were frantically moving their tents," he says.

Like many teams, C.U.B.S. distributes awards at the end of each RAGBRAI. The "Big Thunder Award" went to the loudest snorer, and the "Family Award" was ceremoniously bestowed in absentia on someone who had already left to be with his family. I had no muscle cramps when I biked with this team in 2012, but I was honored with the "Writer's Cramp Award."

Every RAGBRAI, C.U.B.S. treats its members to a one-night hotel stay midweek. This gives everyone the chance to rinse out some laundry and get a good night's sleep. But finding a hotel in a town inundated with twenty thousand RAGBRAIers is always difficult. That's why team leader Brad Prendergast and fellow team member Dana Nelson were working the phones in Des Moines at the 2013 Route Announcement Party. Together with three helpers standing by around the country to contribute ideas and contacts, they snagged a hotel and a country club for their midweek banquet, auction and respite.

SPICY RACK

Although not an official team, a group of lively, animated women trained and rode together in 2012, all wearing the same attention-grabbing jersey labeled "Spicy Rack" across the front. That's not what caught my attention, however. Approaching a member from behind, I noticed an address on the back of her jersey: 2511 Cottage Grove Avenue in Des Moines. Years ago, I lived on Cottage Grove and ate at this location when it housed the Blind Munchies, a laidback restaurant.

The jersey showed that this location is now the home of Woody's Smoke Shack featuring pulled pork, smoked ham and, of course, spicy racks of barbecue ribs. I asked about the restaurant, which sponsors the team, and learned that its owner, Woody Wasson, is an award-winning chef as well as a bicycle fan.

Team Spicy Rack was made up of seven working moms, none of whom lives in Des Moines or works at Woody's, despite promises to "meet you there." They left their

Team Spicy Rack, seven working moms without their husbands or children, got lots of "thumbs up" on RAGBRAI XL. Ringleader Alecia Allen is third from the right. *Alecia Allen.*

husbands and twenty-one children at home for a day because they wanted an adventure of their own. But what a day they picked: the longest day of the week with eighty-five miles and 3,576 feet of climbing. They all completed the ride, although it took some of them twelve hours and several band-aids to do so. Most of the AWOL moms and wives enjoyed the ride enough that they decided to cycle more, on and off RAGBRAI.

Ringleader Alecia Allen (Woody's daughter-in-law) admitted to being a "zero" cyclist prior to RAGBRAI. After the ride, however, the family physician based in Cedar Rapids was planning to occasionally bike to work and even recommend RAGBRAI to some of her patients.

When I asked Allen whether she got any teasing because of her team's name, she replied, "Let's just say we got a lot of thumbs up."

Adaptive Sports Iowa

RAGBRAI is tough enough for able-bodied people. What if you're blind or don't have the use of your legs? No problem, says Mike Boone, director of Adaptive Sports Iowa (ASI), which fielded its first RAGBRAI team in 2011.

Having grown up with a blind father and worked in college as a ski instructor for the disabled, Boone is sensitive to the needs of the disabled. He moved to Des Moines in 2005 and became enthused about RAGBRAI. The three years he rode it on his own, he noticed few cyclists with disabilities so he and his wife, Joni, decided to start ASI, under the auspices of the Iowa Sports Foundation. ASI creates and organizes events for disabled athletes. All its activities are free to participants thanks to donations and sponsorships.

ASI's first RAGBRAI team had twenty-four members, about half disabled athletes and half volunteers. The following year, it fielded fifty-six members, including fourteen riders on hand cycles, two amputees on upright bikes, one amputee on a recliner and two blind cyclists on the back of tandems. Boone says these athletes are among the most inspiring people he's ever met. "Spend five minutes with them, and you'll have a different perspective on life."

That turned out to be an understatement. A car crash left Mike Benge without the use of his legs, but that did not stop him from embracing extreme sports, including off-road mountain biking, which he does on his hands and knees, steering with his chest. "Some trails take me an hour to go forty feet, so I knew I could handle the physical challenges of RAGBRAI," says Benge, who is proud to have completed the entire ride both years.

Michael Hatfield had polio as an infant, but he considers himself "lucky" because his case was not as severe as others, a fact that allows him to get around on braces and

Mike Hatfield leads a line of hand cyclists with Adaptive Sports Iowa, a team for riders with disabilities. *Mike Boone, ASI.*

crutches. "When I see others on RAGBRAI looking at me, I smile and wave or start a conversation so that they won't feel uncomfortable about my disability," Hatfield says.

And Tai Blas sees nothing negative about her blindness, which she says helps her to meet other people. "When you rely on others for a hand every now and then, you get to know lots of great people," she says.

Despite Blas's cheerfulness, disabled riders face many more challenges than other cyclists on RAGBRAI. Their bikes cost more. Most of the kybos and showers are not accessible. Just drinking water or eating a power bar while biking can be difficult when you're pedaling with your hands. In addition, being close to the ground means the temperature is several degrees higher for hand cyclists than for riders on standard bikes. And disabled riders often have to carry more gear, such as the crutches that Hatfield keeps bungee-corded to his hand cycle.

Since many members of ASI can't get into RAGBRAI's sag wagon, the team is allowed to bring one of its vehicles on the bicycle route in case it's needed to help a rider. And because camping is difficult for the disabled, ASI arranges for indoor accommodations each night and provides an air mattress for each team member.

The already generous Iowa hospitality goes into overdrive when it comes to accommodating riders with disabilities. "When word gets out about our team visiting a particular town, we often have people and facilities approach us with free or discounted solutions to our challenges," Boone says.

Members of the ASI team are out to improve the awareness of disabilities and promote an understanding of the issues disabled cyclists face. "We represent the disabled community, and we look at RAGBRAI as a teaching opportunity," says hand cyclist Benge. He loves to sweeten the lesson with a little humor. "Sometimes I tell people that I'm not really disabled—that I just pretend to be in order to get to the front of the line for pie."

Team Livestrong

One of the largest and most visible teams for the past six years has been Team Livestrong, powered by a desire to fight cancer and its affect on survivors, families and friends. When members of this team ride together, their striking yellow and black uniforms burn an indelible image in the mind of everyone who sees them. This is a team with a purpose. This is an army in the War on Cancer.

Even more compelling, this was Lance Armstrong's team. Up until 2012, when Armstrong admitted to doping, this cancer survivor extraordinaire and supposed cycling superstar was a hero to most RAGBRAI riders. That admiration was especially evident during RAGBRAI because Lance's seven Tour de France victories (since rescinded) occurred in July and thus overlapped with RAGBRAI. Engaged in their own grueling bicycle tour, riders took great pleasure in tracking the progress of their man in yellow. And given the time difference, RAGBRAIers often caught their champion's latest feat over a midmorning Bloody Mary. Armstrong's apparent prowess inspired them to keep biking through Iowa's heat and hills, although those hills never came close to the height of Europe's mountains.

The connection to Armstrong propelled Team Livestrong to great heights. Founded in 2007, the team grew to 110 riders and raised a total of $1.3 million, up until and including 2012. Each member was required to raise $1,500 in donations each year. Extremely dedicated teammate Cindy Trent rode with the team each of its six years and raised more than $11,000 in 2012. Having lost six family and extended-family members to cancer, she says that Team Livestrong has developed into "another kind of family" for her.

Teammate Lisa Thomas also started riding in 2007 while undergoing chemotherapy for breast cancer. On the ride in 2012, Team Livestrong celebrated her being cancer free for five years. Teammate Linda Muller became known as the team's "Ribbon

Lady" because she pins ribbons to her jersey with the names of people who had or have cancer.

Christina Anderson rides RAGBRAI as a tribute to her daughter Katie, who died of a brain tumor. In 2007, Christina and Katie, who already had the tumor, happened to see RAGBRAI pass through Lamont. Noticing riders with disabilities, Katie said, "Mom, we should do that." The mother and daughter never got the chance as Katie died shortly thereafter. Still, when RAGBRAI announced in 2010 that the ride would end in Dubuque, Christina's hometown, she decided to do RAGBRAI herself. Christina had not ridden a bike for twenty-five years, but that did not stop her from heading off on a borrowed bike wearing borrowed cycling gear.

Christina did not share her daughter's story with her Livestrong teammates right away, but it came out eventually because what would have been Katie's nineteenth birthday fell within the week of the ride. "The team provides a warm, safe opportunity to share," Christina says.

In fact, Team Livestrong gathers every evening for an unusual "Happy Hour," a time to share stories about cancer that includes tears and laughter, Trent says. "Some of the stories are sad and others are happy, but the evening is always uplifting."

When Christina did the ride in 2010 as a memorial to her daughter, she thought it would be "one and done," but she continues to ride RAGBRAI because Team Livestrong provides a support network, she says. "I see these teammates only one week per year, but I've gotten to know some of them better than most people I see every day."

Whether this camaraderie continues within Team Livestrong remains to be seen. The scandal surrounding Armstrong's doping and denials could detract from the appeal of the Livestrong brand, or it could motivate people to rally around Team Livestrong. "I don't believe Lance's problems will hurt us," Trent says. "This team is not about him but rather about surviving cancer and its effects."

Air Force

Many armed forces field a RAGBRAI team, but Team Air Force always stands out. They outnumber the army, navy and marines, combined, with 100 members in 2012 and more than 150 in other years.

But what really makes them stand out is the way they help other riders. In fact, members of Team Air Force, who usually ride in small groups, make a habit of swooping down on any cyclist in distress. "Within a minute after I got a flat, they came out of nowhere and fixed it for me," says David Borzo (the author's brother) of his ride in 2009. "It was hot, and my recumbent was giving me trouble, so the Air Force was a real godsend."

Team Air Force reported fixing 556 flats during RAGBRAI XL. "They should be called Team repAIR Force," quips David Borzo.

Helping others along the ride is the team mantra. "It's almost an extension of our 'no man left behind' philosophy," says team director Colonel Joseph "Mad Max" Robinson.

"Maybe they should be called Team repAIR Force," David quips.

In 2012, the team reported replacing 396 inner tubes provided by the Air Force and another 160 provided by riders. It also performed more than 270 bike repairs, from minor adjustments to fixing a broken chain, and responded to more than 180 medical situations, including bandaging skinned knees, redirecting traffic and assisting emergency responders.

Team Air Force was formed in 1994, primarily as a recruitment tool. Since Robinson became director in 2004, the primary purpose has evolved into community outreach. "What we want is an opportunity to meet the public and for the public to see who we are," Robinson says. The team also helps keep airmen and airwomen fit to serve.

Senior air force officials have ridden with the team, including generals, former secretaries and, in 1997, the active secretary, Sheila Widnall. Somewhat surprisingly, team members fund their own way, paying for their registration, uniforms, transportation and food. They are not, however, required to take leave to participate. One potential downside of that perk is that they are technically on duty while riding from 6:00 a.m. to 5:00 p.m. Only after 5:00 p.m. are they allowed to have a beer.

Chapter 8

NUTS AND BOLTS

How It Works

RAGBRAI is a monumental enterprise, requiring a full year of preparation and extensive coordination among many parties. With a $5 million budget, it relies on the work of three full-time and one part-time staff positions. Volunteers, many of whom devote hundreds of hours to the venture each year, do the rest of the work.

The job that gets the most attention is choosing the route. Early on, the director would sketch a route across a map, and that was pretty much it. Today, the process is much more involved. The summer before the ride, the director starts to formulate a few potential routes. He asks towns that might serve as overnight communities whether they'd like to be considered. In the meantime, communities that want to host are free to apply or lobby.

A long time ago, RAGBRAI officials had to sell communities on the idea of letting a horde of cyclists invade their towns. No one knew what to expect. "We had to explain that this was not a bunch of motorcycle gangs," says Chuck Offenburger, former RAGBRAI co-host. One year, a local headline read, "Perry Exhales as Bikers Leave," with the story expressing relief that RAGBRAI's visit, "a disaster that never occurred," actually went well.

Town by town, RAGBRAI built up a good reputation. Equally important, it demonstrated its ability to give local economies a shot in the arm. As a result, no arm-twisting is needed anymore.

But choosing a route involves more than connecting the dots on a map of towns willing and able to host. The director considers whether a community has already hosted and, if so, how many times. He also considers how each town seeking to repeat performed in previous years.

The director and his staff calculate the length and climb of each potential route. They don't want a route that's too long or too hilly—nor one that's not long or hilly *enough*. Relying on numbers from www.geobike.com, the authoritative website for

Countless volunteers putting in long hours is what makes RAGBRAI work.

RAGBRAI statistics, the mileage has ranged enormously from 379 miles (1977) to 550 miles (1985). The climb has ranged even more significantly from 10,675 feet (1977) to 26,374 feet (1981).

Throughout their planning, RAGBRAI staffers consult with the Iowa State Patrol, Iowa Department of Transportation, county engineers and local bike clubs about the condition and suitability of roads. Has one road fallen into disrepair? Is another scheduled for resurfacing? Is one road exceptionally busy? Is another particularly scenic?

Whenever possible, paved, low-traffic county roads and state highways are selected. Safety is the main concern followed by scenic beauty. Short sections of gravel and dirt roads are occasionally unavoidable. (If this seems surprising, consider that one-third of U.S. roads—i.e., 1.3 million of 4 million total miles—are covered with gravel or dirt.)

Sometimes the previous route will have a direct bearing on the following one. The 2013 route will be relatively easy because the 2012 ride turned out to be tough. "Forty was so difficult with the heat that anyone who rode it deserves a break on forty-one," says T.J. Juskiewicz, director.

Once the new route is selected, RAGBRAI confirms that the overnight towns are onboard. Years ago, this was done abruptly, about a week before the route was announced.

In 1990, Ardith Lein, head of Sioux Center's chamber of commerce, was surprised to get a call from RAGBRAI coordinator Don Benson, who said, "Greenie, Chuck and I are in Alton. We'll be there in twenty minutes. Get your people together." That meant Sioux Center had been selected as the starting point for RAGBRAI XVIII, but it made Lein, new at her job, anxious. What would it mean to accept their offer? She quickly learned from the mayor that not accepting was not an option.

All of this is done in secrecy so no one gets a head start on hotel reservations in the overnight towns. "I've had more than a few beers bought for me but never divulged the route," Juskiewicz says.

Sergeant Scott Bright, safety education coordinator with the Iowa State Patrol, reports the same pressure when he's been privy due to his role scouting the route. "One year, a state trooper e-mailed me, 'Help out a fellow trooper, brother,' but there's no way I'd ever spill the beans," he says.

The secrecy has spawned a cottage industry around detecting the route because riders want to reserve hotel rooms and secure housing from friends and former hosts before everyone else does. Team Skunk used to follow Benson around Iowa, "driving him mad," says Tim Lane, team founder. When Lane joked about putting a GPS device in *Register* vehicles, RAGBRAI officials started scouting the ride in unmarked cars. Some people tried to guess the route by talking to local sheriffs, reading city council minutes from around the state and checking which hotels were booked during the week of the ride.

In early 2008, RAGBRAI staffers were getting ready to tell city officials in Le Claire that it had been selected as the last town for RAGBRAI XXXVI. As with all the overnight towns, it was going to ask Le Clair to keep the news a secret until it was announced in the *Register* a few days later. As the team arrived, however, it noticed TV trucks outside the building. "We kept driving and called the *Register*, telling them to release the news immediately," says Jim Green, RAGBRAI coordinator. "That's when we decided that there had to be a better way of revealing the carefully guarded secret."

That better idea, a Route Announcement Party, was copied from Cycle Oregon and launched in 2010. The Iowa Bicycle Coalition co-hosts the party in Des Moines in late January as a fundraiser. Attracting more than one thousand people, the gala includes a silent auction, VIP reception, light dinner and live music. It's preceded by a large bike expo during the day.

The buildup to the long-awaited announcement is exciting. Many attendees spread maps across their tables, ready to hit the phones to find lodging the moment each overnight town is announced.

Another important function that RAGBRAI performs is running a lottery for registrants. As the number of riders swelled from 150 in year one to 4,000 in year four (with unofficial estimates running as high as 500 and 6,000, respectively), something had to be done to check the ride's growth. By 1982, RAGBRAI had capped the number of riders who could register at 5,500 and created a drawing to allocate the

RAGBRAI's main campgrounds are always carefully choreographed. *Photo by Dave McWhinnie.*

spots. And in 1986, it started issuing I.D. wristbands that would give riders access to designated campsites and make them eligible for support services, including medical and sag; free admission to events; and discounts on food, beverages, showers, bike repair and merchandise.

For weeklong registration, RAGBRAI adopted a lottery rather than first-come, first-served to help people from outside Iowa have a better chance of participating. That seems to work, as at least 60 percent are out-of-staters most years. RAGBRAI has experimented with different caps, settling in 2000 on 8,500 for the week plus 1,500 for each day. It hands out 1,500 vehicle passes, as well.

When RAGBRAI introduced the lottery, existing teams, including Silver Streaks, Tall Dog Bike Club and Bicyclists of Iowa City were grandfathered in with a certain number of guaranteed spots. For instance, Team Skunk gets 120 wristbands and two vehicle passes. Members of teams created after the lottery have to take their chances on the drawing. Most years, applications exceed available spots. RAGBRAI reported turning away more than 4,000 applicants in 1987 and many more in other years, including more than 7,000 in 1990, which led to ticket scalping. Today, however, most applicants are accepted under the 8,500 limit, according to Juskiewicz.

RAGBRAI strongly encourages all riders to register, but up to 12,000 at a time jump onto the route unregistered, especially in and out of big cities. To encourage everyone, including day-trippers, to register, RAGBRAI introduced one-day wristbands in 1996, sold first-come, first-served.

COMMITTEES STEP UP

Once the route is announced, overnight towns and the ending town organize committees and start raising money, with the chamber of commerce usually taking the lead. First they select an advisory board, five to seven well-connected people. This board chooses up to four co-chairs to spearhead the day-to-day efforts. Co-chairs, together with a secretary and treasurer, make up the town's RAGBRAI Executive Committee.

Each member of the executive committee is encouraged to take responsibility for four or five of the nineteen committees that cover specific areas: beverage garden; budget; campgrounds; communications; electrical; entertainment and special events; food and vendors; hospitality; housing; information center; law enforcement; medical; publicity; public safety; Ride Right, a safety program; showers, sanitation and recycling; transportation; volunteers; and web and social media.

This long list gives an idea of the vast and varied amount of work that goes into hosting the twenty thousand or more cyclists and supporters. This huge, multifaceted undertaking can severely tax the time and talents of local communities, especially considering that many small-town residents are deeply engaged in family, church, clubs, community groups and civic organizations. Let's just say it's hard to find a babysitter when RAGBRAI comes to town.

RAGBRAI distributes a three-hundred-page handbook that explains the role of every person and committee. It offers advice and conducts workshops; provides a CD with templates for useful documents, forms and maps; and sets detailed timelines and checklists.

Two important initial tasks for each executive committee are creating a budget and drafting a special citywide ordinance to deal with issues associated with a RAGBRAI visit, including the sale and distribution of alcohol, hours of operation, location of operations and vendor fees. Such ordinances are aimed at clarifying expectations and giving law enforcement a tool to keep things under control and shut down unlicensed vendors.

To help accomplish everything on time, RAGBRAI staffers visit each host town frequently, guiding them through the planning process and implementation phase. This work keeps the director crisscrossing the state for months. Besides relying on RAGBRAI staff for assistance, committee members from host towns often call on their counterparts in other towns, some of whom have years of RAGBRAI experience. Joshua Schamberger, president of the Iowa City/Coralville Area Convention and

Visitors Bureau, has a multidimensional perspective. Not only has he worked four RAGBRAIs, but he's also ridden nine of them.

While the local committees are whipping the overnight towns into shape, the RAGBRAI director fine-tunes the route by selecting the pass-through towns. When these are announced in March, the pass-through towns begin a similar but less rigorous preparation process. They don't have to worry about campgrounds and showers, but they still have to deal with traffic, alcohol, entertainment, medical and other issues.

RAGBRAI also designates a vehicle route for the cars, trucks, buses and vans that support the riders. The vehicle route intersects with the bicycle route at meet-up towns, which are designated towns for riders and their supporters to connect midday.

BEVERAGE COMMITTEE/BEER GARDEN

The towns' committee work can be tense and demanding, and the beverage committee often generates the most controversy. Residents of conservative Sioux Center initially opposed a beer garden the first time that city hosted in 1990, but they gradually

RAGBRAI often turns Main Street into a pedestrian mall. Here it's party time in Mount Vernon on RAGBRAI XL.

accepted the idea, deciding that it was better to concentrate the drinking in one place, where it could be better controlled.

The beverage committee is usually the only one that has the potential to generate significant income, $70,000 or more. Sometimes it pays for everything involved with hosting and generates a handsome profit for the town and/or operator.

A brief look at the responsibilities of the beverage garden committee will demonstrate the scale and complexity of preparing for RAGBRAI. If the beverage garden, aka beer garden, is run by a civic organization, that organization must acquire a liquor license. At the same time, licensed establishments in town should be discouraged from operating a beverage garden in competition.

Preventing minors from drinking is one of the biggest challenges the committee faces. Many techniques for doing this have been developed. Double fencing prevents adults inside from passing drinks to minors outside. Having no more than two entrances makes it easier to control access, and having them well lighted helps volunteers read identification cards. Staffing the entrances with local high school teachers and counselors discourages minors from trying to enter with a false I.D.

Liability, fire and dram shop insurance are required while rain insurance is recommended. A certain number of toilets will be mandated, and the Americans with Disabilities Act calls for a certain number of them to be accessible.

Choosing a location can be tricky. Fire regulations require ten square feet per person, so if five thousand people are expected to attend, the beverage garden needs to be the size of a football field! But a beverage garden must not be too close to the campground, which is a quiet zone after 9:00 p.m. And it should be closed by midnight, since riders need to hit the road the next morning.

Pass-through towns have beverage gardens, too, which can lead to heavy drinking and loud music in the morning or afternoon. These towns have agreed to close their beverage gardens and other drinking establishments by a certain time to enable riders to reach the day's destination by 6:00 p.m., when support services are discontinued. Nevertheless, sometimes these agreements are not followed. The penultimate towns each day, which attract partiers, can be the worst violators.

Then there's the cleanup. RAGBRAI requires that the area be cleared of litter and debris by 4:00 a.m. because cyclists may pass through on their way out of town.

And on and on. You get the idea; running a beer garden is surprisingly complicated.

Other committees have their share of issues to deal with. Somehow all the work gets done. It did in Manchester in 1999, when three teens co-chaired the Hospitality Committee. On the other end of the age spectrum, Hanover Historical Village's fifteen-member board, most of them in their seventies, formed ready-made RAGBRAI committees in 2012.

Since Hanover is a restored historical site with three residents, the board was worried about how to manage thousands of RAGBRAIers. Thanks to a tremendous volunteer

Hanover Historical Village demonstrated old farm equipment and showcased its general store on RAGBRAI XL. It had been taken off the map in the 1960s but now, with a population of three, it's back on.

effort, things went extremely well. "We hired pancake and other food vendors and supplemented that with popcorn, bananas, Rice Krispies bars and other items," said Marilyn Hinkeldey, who served on the food and vendors committee. "Some things surprised us, like riders asking for a hamburger at 8:00 a.m., but I guess that was lunchtime for them."

About nine thousand riders stopped at Hanover, a town that all but died in the 1960s but was resuscitated in the 1990s by the historical society. The riders were well nourished and enjoyed the historical buildings, exhibits and demonstrations. In so doing, they left a lot of money behind that will be used to continue the village's educational programs and renovate its buildings and equipment. "We're ready to do this all over again!" Hinkeldey says.

OTHER SERVICES

RAGBRAI staffers also have to make sure the route they choose is safe and adequate. Starting in the fall, they conduct inspection trips by car. Local bike clubs help check the route, too. In June, RAGBRAI officials bike the entire route, accompanied by friends and supporters, to get a two-wheel perspective on the road surfaces, hills, turns, amenities and intersections. After each scouting trip, the parties report road hazards and suggest improvements to state, county and local officials. Typically, these problems are corrected, at least as far as budgets allow.

Once the ride starts, other services kick into gear: bike receiving and shipping stations, information centers, parking, signage, lost and found, first-aid and four ambulances and paramedic teams that patrol the route. During the early years, one open sag wagon brought up the rear. Today, four air-conditioned vans work the route, each one pulling a trailer for fifteen bikes. RAGBRAI insists participants should be prepared to bike the entire route and not consider the sag wagon a taxi service.

Many riders sag with their team's support vehicles, but the official sag wagon is rarely used, except in extreme weather conditions. On "Saggy Thursday" in 1995, when a thirty-five-mile-per-hour headwind kicked in, RAGBRAI sagged an estimated one-third of the cyclists. On days like this, RAGBRAI procures extra trucks and buses. On one of the hotter days in 2012, director Juskiewicz called on Pork Belly Ventures, a charter with a large fleet, to help sag about one thousand riders.

Teams, charters and ten official bike shops offer repair services along the route, in host towns and at campgrounds. *Photo by Bob Frank, PBV.*

RAGBRAI

Currently, RAGBRAI contracts with ten official bike shops, all based in Iowa: Bike Country, Ankeny; Connecticut Yankee Pedaller, Chariton; Letsche's Bike Shop, Cherokee; Boulevard Sports, Des Moines; Bikes to You, Grinnell; Harper's Cycling and Fitness, Muscatine; Rider Sales, Washington; Bike World, Ames; Rasmussen Bike Shop, West Des Moines; and Spoken Wheel Cyclery, Iowa Falls. Every day, they set up in and between overnight towns on a rotating basis.

"We don't make much money on RAGBRAI because we charge the same prices as we do in our stores, even though we have a higher overhead on the ride," says Forrest Ridgway, owner of Bike World and a RAGBRAI veteran going back to 1974, when he worked as a mechanic for Bill's Cyclery. "We do it for the PR and to support RAGBRAI."

Sophisticated, high-end bikes can be tough to service on the ride, he adds. "Components are not interchangeable, like they were in the early days of RAGBRAI. Nevertheless, with overnight shipping, we're able to get odd parts quickly and take care of just about everything."

The days are long, says Tom Healy, a Bike World mechanic from 2005 to 2012. He sleeps in a windowless trailer with all the bike parts, saying, "It's hot but sleeping there is easier than setting up and taking down a tent every day, especially since we have to be on the road by four-thirty some mornings."

In addition to directing traffic, Iowa State Patrol troopers blast music for riders' enjoyment. Talk about the Party Patrol!

Bicycle manufacturers also accompany the ride, often with loaner bikes that riders can test ride. If a cyclist wants to keep the loaner all day, the manufacturer will typically transport his or her bicycle to the next overnight town. In 2005, Cannondale brought forty bikes on RAGBRAI, and by the end of the week, 250 riders had tried them out.

The most important issue RAGBRAI works on is safety, Juskiewicz says. RAGBRAI works closely with the Iowa State Patrol, without which the ride would not be possible. Realizing that the event offered a great public relations opportunity, the patrol jumped on board in 1974, a time when law enforcement was not widely revered due to the turbulent 1960s and Kent State shootings of 1970.

Trooper Bill Zenor, who has been involved with RAGBRAI since 1974, set the service bar high. Always helpful and usually amusing, Zenor kept order and encouraged riders to keep up their spirits. After retiring from the force, he served as RAGBRAI's safety coordinator for many years.

Today, the patrol helps choose the route, promotes safety and advises on other matters. Once the ride starts, troopers direct traffic and enforce liquor laws. For the past several years, troopers also have swept through each town to see that the bars and beer garden are closed and to encourage bikers to continue. "If we don't keep them moving, town by town, chances are they'll end up impaired, riding after dark without lights," Juskiewicz says. "We don't want anyone to get hit by a semi!"

The troopers project a friendly, supportive attitude, bantering with the riders and blasting rock music from their patrol cars for the enjoyment of passing cyclists. Any complaints? "We get about nine thousand 'thank yous' every day, which gets a little old, but we very much appreciate the gratitude and respect," Bright says. "Standing in the heat or rain for twelve hours is a tough job. The temperature of the pavement has been measured as high as 126 degrees."

Team Gourmet's William McGhie is in trouble again! (Not really.) Troopers keep things under control on RAGBRAI. *Janet Kersey Kowal.*

In the past, troopers took turns riding a tandem across the state. "Nowadays, resources are stretched too thin for that, but troopers love the ride," Bright says. "Active troopers have been known to take the week off to ride. We're on a first-name basis with many riders."

CHARTER SERVICES

How RAGBRAI unfolds for cyclists depends, in large measure, on what they choose from a wide variety of riding and housing options ranging from self-contained camping to hotel accommodations.

Most riders used RAGBRAI's baggage truck to transport their gear. In an effort to limit the number of riders, the *Register* announced in 1975 that it would carry baggage for only the first 2,500 riders who signed up. This prompted riders to arrange their own baggage transport. It also led to more vehicles and services, including charters. By 1978, a veritable procession of vehicles was accompanying the cyclists across the state.

By 2013, RAGBRAI was planning to carry bags for only about 1,500 riders, less than one-fifth of the total. Teams and charters have assumed much of the logistics, and RAGBRAI is happy with that. Not only do these private entities carry the baggage and find campsites, but they also feed, entertain, monitor and control their riders.

Opposite, top: Members of large groups and those using the *Register*'s baggage service sometimes have to search a while for their bags. *Photo by Bob Frank.*

Right: RAGBRAI is more than a bike ride. Camping is also a challenge, but teams and charters make it easier. This is Pork Belly Ventures' Sioux City campground in 2010. *Photo by Bob Frank.*

RAGBRAI

RAGBRAI's registration fee had risen to $150 by 2013. Going with RAGBRAI's baggage and camping service is inexpensive but has a few drawbacks. The main campground tends to be noisy. Showers are often lukewarm and typically require a long walk or shuttle from the site. And finding one's bag in the pile of bags that RAGBRAI deposits at the main campground can be difficult. (In 2000, one camper placed a wireless, remote-controlled doorbell in his bag, but the idea didn't catch on.) Once campers find their bags, they have to carry them back to the campsite and set up their own tents. As a result, riders have been increasingly signing up with teams and charters that provide more services, albeit at a cost.

Charters are similar to teams, but they are run for-profit by tour companies, bike shops and others. For 2013, RAGBRAI sanctioned twenty charters (see http://ragbrai.com/about/charter-services). The charter operators are a collegial bunch even though they often compete for the same customers. The largest by far is Pork Belly Ventures (PBV), with 970 weeklong customers and 1,350 total customers in 2012.

Pete Phillips founded PBV in 1994. He and Tammy Pavich, his business partner since 1995, had run and worked on other RAGBRAI charters prior to that. Both know RAGBRAI intimately. Phillips biked his first RAGBRAI in 1986, and Pavich biked her first one in 1984. The year 2013 will mark Pavich's thirtieth consecutive one (as a rider or worker).

In its first year, PBV had ninety-five customers, a paper-based mailing list and not much else. Today, it's ten times as big and much more sophisticated. The story of its growth shows how charters have developed and reflects how RAGBRAIers, themselves, have changed, seeking evermore amenities and comforts.

In the beginning, PBV rented trucks every year and built temporary shelves in them to hold supplies. Now it hauls baggage, bikes and other supplies in its own fleet. In the beginning, PBV would brew coffee each night in a one-hundred-cup coffeemaker and keep it warm (sort of) in thermoses until the next morning. Now it has a beverage truck with electric power that provides gallons of hot beverages every morning.

About ten years ago, when PBV noticed its clients searching for a place to plug in their cellphones, it attached a power strip to a generator. The following year it built a device with 100 outlets, followed the next year by one with 260 outlets. In 2013, PBV rolled out a custom-made, sixteen-foot, walk-in trailer with 750 private lockers, each containing two outlets. (The lockers are not for security, but rather to prevent mistaking one similar-looking phone or camera for another.)

The handyman behind these innovations is Phillips, a full-time firefighter who devotes most of his free time to designing and building the charter's customized trailers and devices (or "thingies," as they're called). Pavich handles the administration and communications, the latter of which includes about thirty group e-mails to their customers prior to each ride. (Good thing she has a PhD in English.)

Catering to cyclists' increasing needs and expectations, some teams and charters provide recharging stations, tent concierge services and hot coffee in the morning. *Photo by Bob Frank, PBV.*

PBV has ten trailers (one of which opens into a stage): the aforementioned coffee and recharging trailers; two for baggage; two for showers; one for bikes; a restroom trailer with six flushing toilets and six urinals; and two fifty-two-foot, air-conditioned motel trailers. Introduced in 2011, the first of these five-room motel trailers sold out in minutes. Each room sleeps up to four and rents for $2,500 per week. PBV could charge a lot more but instead requires a $200 donation per room to the Juvenile Diabetes Foundation.

At the other end of the charter's price spectrum is $15 for a ride to RAGBRAI's starting town. Full, weeklong participants paid $395 in 2013, not counting RAGBRAI's $150 fee.

PBV's large size allows it to offer things that smaller charters cannot afford, such as nightly entertainment and thirty-five shower stalls. About six years ago it started to rent and set up tents, and that contributed greatly to its growth. Pavich says she never expected PBV to grow so big. "Several times, we tried to cap our numbers, but people would say, 'My cousin can get off work after all,' or 'I came last year; can't I come this year?' Eventually we decided to take all comers."

Despite all its equipment, expertise and eighty-member crew, PBV has never worked another event. That may change soon, as it plans to develop its own events and send shower trailers to the Bicycle Ride Across Nebraska.

Pavich and Phillips have heart. Every year, they help a local Iowa church by buying dinner at the church for their entire charter group and then having the church rent its pews to riders who wouldn't mind paying a few bucks to sleep in rain-free, air-conditioned comfort for one night. Heavenly!

They also have a sense of humor. They used to bring the ugliest couch they could find and use it as a campsite centerpiece each year. They've rented a piglet as the charter's pet. And they decorate their trailers with amusing sayings, such as "High on the Hog," "Pass the Corn" and "It's Not So Much the Heat. It's the Stupidity."

Charters and teams depend on an army of support staffers who drive the trucks, buses and vans; schlep bags; pitch and break down tents; shop; fetch ice; set up showers; fill shower bags with water; post route signs; prepare food and drinks at campsites; clean up campsites; massage sore muscles; and shuttle riders to and from town. They also give directions, answer endless questions, report weather forecasts, share their cellphones and perform myriad other tasks. After all this, many of them take on their most important task: getting off to an early start the next morning to stake out a good campsite. Working behind the scenes, these troops are usually underappreciated. Even so, they're essential.

A little-discussed fact is that crews will often sag cyclists part or all of the way on some days, especially days with long miles and high hills. Old-timers lament that this happens more and more, but there are more vehicles on RAGBRAI, including five hundred RVs registered in 2012, so many riders can easily find a lift, at least part of the way.

The Czech Plus Polka Band entertains at the campground of Pork Belly Ventures, a charter known for funny sayings on its trucks, including "High on the hog" and "Pork Place." *Photo by Bob Frank, PBV.*

RAGBRAI depends on support crews, such as this one working for Pork Belly Ventures in 2012. *Photo by Bob Frank, PBV.*

As on a cruise or at the health club, a massage is usually close at hand on RAGBRAI. *Photo by Bob Frank, PBV.*

Support staffers tend to be well paid, especially with tips. Joe Petermeier, a crewmember for the Iowa Valley Bicycle Club, says he made $1,700 in 2012. But the main attraction for him was the fun and experience. "I like the event," he says. "It's amazing to see how many people bike that far. The best part is the people. I felt integrated with the team, even though I didn't ride."

Finding and keeping a good crew, or at least a good crew chief, is challenging, partly because after seeing the ride up close many of the workers want to return as cyclists. In fact, cycling RAGBRAI might be easier than lugging heavy bags, some of which weigh ninety pounds, despite limits of forty or fifty pounds that most teams suggest.

Chapter 9

SHIFT HAPPENS

When Things Go Wrong

Planning, organizing and managing an event of RAGBRAI's size and scale is challenging. Over the years there have been serious problems, both immediate crises and long-term difficulties.

Ironically, the editor of the very newspaper that sponsors RAGBRAI brought about its darkest day. On August 1, 1980, an article appeared in the *Register* that portrayed RAGBRAI as full of sex and drugs. Among other things, the story mentioned "animal acts," "good dope," "anything goes" and "intertwined couples seeking late-night freedom from the constraints of their tents."

"By night, a goodly number of [riders]—mostly the people from 18 to 30—mass in the bars seeking just the right person to share a tent," it read. "Indeed, the main thing a young man needs for this ride is not a good bicycle, insists a tan and smiling 27-year-old…The tent, the music, the refreshments and the marijuana all but assure he will have companionship each night, he says."

No one knows why Gartner took a cheap shot at RAGBRAI. The day he wrote this story, the riders were engaged in a 114-mile ride with 2,573 feet of climbing, one-third of the way into a headwind. While Gartner picked up on sex and drugs, other journalists were writing about how tough RAGBRAI riders were. *Register* reporter Jim Blume wrote that RAGBRAI riders are "consumed by an unnatural desire to cross every bridge, climb every hill and scoff at every shortcut." He went on to quote Dave Lowenberg of West Point, saying, "The most important part is the feeling of accomplishment when you reach the campground."

Would the newspaper's copyeditors have toned down or cut Gartner's article if it had been written by anyone other than their boss's boss?

The article set off a maelstrom of protests. Many riders worried they would have "a lot of 'splainin' to do" when they got home to their families. Others contradicted Gartner's characterization of the ride to anyone who would listen. Some, however, opted to live up to Gartner's description of raucous behavior. Partying and drinking escalated throughout the day the article appeared.

The overnight town that day was Elkader (population 1,688). Things got rowdy as it filled up with six thousand or more cyclists and an undetermined number of locals curious about all the supposed "sex and drugs." Many people drank too much, and a few streaked, mooned and climbed buildings.

"We saw all day that things were getting increasingly out of hand, and the problems escalated at Elkader," says Tim Lane, founder of Team Skunk. "As a kind of toast, people were spilling beer on riders when they arrived. And people were drinking and dancing in the street, which blocked traffic."

That street was Highway 13, which went through the middle of Elkader and was not supposed to be a part of the festivities. Nevertheless, it remained packed for hours. The action was centered on a bar on that street. It was impossible to tell whether locals or cyclists were more raucous, but some people were itching for a fight. The mood turned dangerous.

At one point, the police and state troopers decided to clear the street. At least one trooper wanted to do so with billy clubs swinging, but cooler heads prevailed. With the help of plainclothes officers and members of Team Skunk, the officers successfully moved the party around the corner onto the street that had been designated for RAGBRAI revelers. Many who rode that year say the incident came close to getting ugly but that moving the crowd dissolved the tension.

The immediate fallout of that rowdy night in Elkader was minimal because no fights broke out and no arrests were made. In addition, the incident occurred on the last night of the ride. The next morning, RAGBRAI took off for Guttenberg, an easy twenty-five miles away, and everyone went home.

All the same, Gartner's article and ensuing reactions left a lot of hurt feelings as well as a new realization that RAGBRAI could crash and burn. "Gartner almost shut down RAGBRAI singlehandedly," says Janet Kersey Kowal, who rode that year as a teenager. "His article was discussed all over the campground that night—seriously and mockingly. One camper would call out, 'Got any pot over there?' and another one would answer, 'Quiet down; we're having sex.'"

Over the next few days, criticism of Gartner was unanimous. Dave Yoder wrote in the *Perry Daily Chief*: "I was shocked and amazed to hear that the thousands of bikers who stopped in Perry on July 29 were actually engaged in an orgy of drugs and sex. It came as a surprise to many of the bikers on the trip as well as to two-time veterans like myself. I don't know where Michael Gartner collected his information, but it was nowhere I had ever been on the ride."

Karras wrote, "It always has struck me that spending eight or ten hours crushing the pudendal nerve on an unforgiving bicycle seat is hardly conducive to passionate behavior." And Kaul wrote, "The week is still one of long-distance biking and lemonade," adding that the drug of choice for the week was aspirin.

College towns usually make great host communities. Mount Vernon, home of Cornell College, pulled out all the stops for RAGBRAI XL.

All this is not to say that RAGBRAI is a temperance meeting. Some participants learned their manners from *Animal House*. For them, drinking and carousing are part of the experience. In 1996, Team Gumby, Cheddarheads and Team Cucumber were barred from returning to RAGBRAI after repeated warnings for misconduct. But rowdiness spikes some years and falls off in others. In Glenwood, there were broken beer bottles, nudity and arrests for public intoxication in 1989 but no such disturbances in 1992. Year by year, town by town, the nature and tone of RAGBRAI depends on the operation of the beer garden, local law enforcement, style of entertainment and mood of participants—riders and locals.

Passed Over Town

Another famous brouhaha was also instigated by RAGBRAI itself and developed into one of the event's most controversial disputes. In 2001, the announced route for Tuesday went from Denison to Atlantic, including the pass-through town of Marne (population 149). Less than two weeks before the start of the ride, RAGBRAI announced that instead of following U.S. Highway 83 from Walnut to Marne to Atlantic, the new route would take a couple of county roads and bypass Marne.

RAGBRAI coordinator Jim Green said the change was made for safety reasons. The county roads had been the first choice because they had one-third the traffic volume as Highway 83, he explained. A planned construction project on one of the county roads, however, forced the ride to take the busier Highway 83 instead. But after the construction project on the county road was postponed, RAGBRAI reverted to the preferred route—a route RAGBRAI had followed each of the three previous times it had overnighted in Atlantic.

Many people objected to the last-minute change, which left Marne with expenditures that it would not recoup, including hundreds of dollars on permits and insurance for its beverage garden. In fact, Randy Fischer, chief of Marne's volunteer fire department, told the *Register* he suspected that RAGBRAI officials had rerouted the ride because of the planned beer garden. Marne was only 7.2 miles from Atlantic, and a beer garden that close to the overnight town would have encouraged big drinkers to party hard, knowing they were close to finishing for the day. Meanwhile, it was uncertain whether Marne would agree to close the beer garden at 5:00 p.m., RAGBRAI's deadline so that riders could get to Atlantic by 6:00 p.m., when all RAGBRAI services are discontinued.

"[RAGBRAI] is concerned that people are going to stop in Marne and have too much to drink, and then it's going to be difficult for them to get to Atlantic," Fischer said. "Why didn't they tell me that three months ago?"

Other Marne residents told the *Register* that the beer garden had refused to close by 5:00 p.m., as RAGBRAI wanted it to do.

Whatever the reason for the route change, Marne printed buttons and T-shirts saying, "Marne, Iowa. The pass thru town that got passed by! RAW DEAL BIKE RIDE 2001." In a show of support, members of Atlantic's local RAGBRAI organizing committee threatened to take the unprecedented step of withdrawing as an overnight town. That sent RAGBRAI officials scurrying for an alternative. Within a few days, however, Atlantic backed down.

In the end, the ride bypassed Marne. Ironically, Marne was still on the official maps and merchandise, including maps published in newspapers announcing that Marne would not be on the route. There had been no time to create new maps.

Several hundred riders cycled off the official route through Marne to support the tiny town. "My girlfriend and I felt Marne had been wronged, so we stopped there and spent some money," says Ginny Procuniar. "We were glad to see that they attracted a good crowd."

RAGBRAI's fears about Marne's beer garden were somewhat confirmed by the fact that many cyclists who went off the route to Marne that day were still drinking there as late as 9:00 p.m., four hours after it would have been closed if the ride had gone through Marne.

RAGBRAI

RAGBRAI never passed through Marne again and did not return to Atlantic until ten years later, even though Atlantic had been an overnight town four times in the first nineteen years. In all likelihood, neither action was a coincidence. RAGBRAI officials probably wanted to send a message about closing beer gardens in a timely manner.

CRASHES AND DEATHS

Of course, the biggest RAGBRAI tragedies are deaths during the ride, but there have been surprisingly few. "An exact number is hard to determine, but the semi-official count is twenty-six, with only five fatalities resulting from an accident while someone was actually bicycling," said RAGBRAI director T.J. Juskiewicz. "That's a relatively small number when you consider that RAGBRAI is like a city of twelve thousand people moving across the state, and when you take into account all the riders, all the years, all the miles involved."

The other twenty-one deaths have been caused by a variety of things, mostly heart attacks and then strokes. Participants have also drowned, died in their sleep of natural causes and been killed in car crashes.

On a five-hundred-mile bike ride, there are bound to be many road hazards, such as railroad tracks, potholes, gravel and lateral cracks in the pavement.

One thing that has kept the number of fatalities down and minimized the impact of serious injuries is the remarkable number of nurses, physicians, paramedics and other medical personnel who ride, according to Bob Libby, RAGBRAI's medical director. In 1996, Linda Schlak was bumped off her bike by another cyclist and fell to the shoulder of the road. Two doctors and a nurse were already treating her by the time her husband, with whom she was riding, cycled up. And the forty-nine-year-old Les Cleveland was struggling up a long hill when his heart stopped, and he fell over. A physician cycling behind him started CPR and saved him.

Minor accidents and ailments are all too common, Juskiewicz says, calling the medical crews "the busiest guys on the route." They treat hundreds of cases a day of sunburn, saddle sores, road rash and sore muscles. Broken bones, dehydration, heat stroke and heart ailments occur, but much less frequently.

RAGBRAI officials say most accidents could be avoided if participants would refrain from dangerous behavior, such as drinking too much, stopping in the middle of the road, texting while riding, wearing earplugs to talk on the phone or listen to music, weaving through the mass of cyclists and riding in the dark without lights.

The most dangerous behavior is drafting, in which two or more bicycles ride in a line to cut down on wind resistance. "More than 70 percent of serious but nonfatal injuries are caused by cycle-to-cycle crashes, and the majority of those are related to pace lines," Dan McKay, Ride Right chairperson, told team representatives at a meeting in 2013. "The problem with pace lines is that most RAGBRAI riders don't know how to draft."

McKay recounted a recent crash where eighteen riders living life in the fast lane went down almost instantly after one cyclist swerved into their path. Years earlier, *Register* columnist Donald Kaul put it aptly when he speculated that it must have been a cyclist who invented the Domino Theory.

As long as RAGBRAI attracts so many inexperienced cyclists, Ride Right will have its work cut out because the biggest factor behind accidents on the ride is the inexperience of cyclists, according to a Centers for Disease Control and Prevention survey. During the 2000 ride, crashes and near misses were more common among riders who had less than seven years of regular riding experience than those who had more than seven years.

BANNED IN CRAWFORD COUNTY

The most notorious of RAGBRAI's five bicycling-related deaths occurred in Crawford County in 2004 when Kirk Ullrich was thrown from his bike after his front wheel got caught in a centerline crack.

RAGBRAI

His wife sued the county, saying that it had not adequately maintained the road or warned cyclists about the hazard. In 2007, Crawford County admitted no wrongdoing but settled out of court for $350,000. (The state also paid a settlement.) In response, Crawford County banned RAGBRAI and similar events from using its roads due to liability concerns. Later, Denison, Crawford County's seat, followed suit.

While Iowa law affords bicycles the same rights to the road as motor vehicles, the ban prompted other counties to consider similar action or require organized bike rides to buy exorbitantly priced liability insurance to cover their riders.

In late 2007, the Iowa State Association of Counties (ISAC) proposed a model ordinance aimed at protecting cities and counties from liability for injuries and damages caused by bicycle accidents. The tone and conditions of the proposed ordinance angered bicycle advocates, especially since it began with this statement: "County roads are not designed for bicycles."

If other counties had followed Crawford County's lead or passed ISAC's ordinance, it could have limited or shut down RAGBRAI. Instead, in 2008 RAGBRAI revised its liability waiver to release local governments from liability for the ride. This prompted Crawford County to rescind its ban.

Today, no counties ban RAGBRAI, but many post warning signs during RAGBRAI saying that common conditions, such as centerline cracks and rumble strips, may be hazardous to cyclists. "Bike at your own risk," seems to be the message. For its part, RAGBRAI requires cyclists to sign a waiver (online since 2012) stating that RAGBRAI is not liable for injuries, losses or damages.

Chapter 10

RAGBRAI INSPIRES...ROMANCE, ART, OTHER RIDES, ETC.

ROMANCE

RAGBRAI has a romantic side. Every route is dotted with picturesque places that could be described as a "bicycle stop built for two." As a result, many people pair up, propose and get married—sometimes on RAGBRAI. Others renew their vows or spend their honeymoons on the ride.

In 1998, Kevin Leyen proposed to Carla Van Deest with signs along the route. She said "yes" and was soon displaying an engagement ring with a gold band, tiny bicycle and good-size diamond.

One of the most famous RAGBRAI weddings took place in Atlantic in 1989 when the town went all out to help Mike Albers and his bride, Kim, tie the knot. It provided dinner for four, entertainment, a horse-and-buggy ride, cake, champagne and a hotel room. The city park was packed for the well-publicized ceremony. The next time RAGBRAI overnighted in Atlantic in 2001, the Albers returned to celebrate their anniversary.

Many RAGBRAI weddings forgo the traditional champagne and wedding cake in favor of beer and corn on the cob. Often, the happy couple will be decked out in spandex and bicycle shoes. In 1992, Jame Neagle and Bobbi Wilson even wore their helmets when they got married in Knoxville.

Simple and laid back as they are, RAGBRAI weddings can be stressful. It's easy to forget or misplace the rings when you camp for several days before the wedding. When Geana Allen and Carl Werve got married on RAGBRAI XL, family and friends had to participate via conference call. And Marty McDougall and Beth Wilson were almost late for their wedding in 1995 because it took longer than expected to bike the sixty-nine miles from Onawa to Lake View. With friends and family waiting, they arrived with only minutes to spare.

Tomas Finn and Regina Boutwell tie the knot in Mount Vernon on RAGBRAI XL.

Lorri Wilson and Greg Reed biked even farther to their RAGBRAI wedding. Greg was Lorri's daughter's soccer coach. One day after practice, he asked her if she had ever thought about riding RAGBRAI. "It's on my bucket list," she replied. So Lorri joined Greg's team, and they trained together.

One thing led to another, and by the time they decided to get married, they realized that on the Tuesday during RAGBRAI XXXII their team, Mardi Gras, would be overnighting in Iowa Falls, which was planning a Mardi Gras theme. "It only seemed fitting that we join our lives together on that day, and with a Mardi Gras theme of our own," Lorri says.

They rode the entire week, throwing bachelor and bachelorette parties on Monday, getting married on Tuesday—after biking 100.4 miles, including the Karras Loop—and honeymooning the rest of the week. The wedding took place on the Scenic City Empress Riverboat, and guests were served walking tacos and wedding cake, among other things. A group of cyclists along the shore sang, "Going to the Chapel" a cappella. Afterward, the newlyweds partied in Iowa Falls and ended up on stage with the main entertainment to throw their garter, bouquet and Mardi Gras beads into the crowd. "We did get a late start the next day," Lorri admits. They rode much of the remainder of the week with wedding baseball caps.

Since then, the Reeds have ridden every RAGBRAI and celebrated their anniversary on the ride whenever it fell in that week. "We expect to keep doing this until God says we can't," Lorri says.

Team Rah Rah had a bachelorette party on RAGBRAI in 2009. The bridesmaids appeared to be having a good time celebrating the last week of freedom for one of their members. Their T-shirts said, "We have ways of improving your performance."

The RAGBRAI experience can be good or bad for a couple. Kelli Mullin broke up with her boyfriend two days into RAGBRAI XXIII. "He didn't like the ride and got sick," she told the *Register*. "I realized I could either pamper him or go on ahead. I went on ahead." Meanwhile, on some teams the tandem is known as a "divorce-mobile," and couples who buy one are advised to sign up for marriage counseling.

Kenneth "King Kenny" Groezinger says his wife encourages him to ride

Lorri Wilson and Greg Reed, of Team Mardi Gras, had a Mardi Gras wedding on Tuesday during RAGBRAI XXXII in Iowa Falls, which had a Mardi Gras theme. *Laissez les bon temps rouler! Lorri Reed.*

RAGBRAI and always takes advantage of his absence to work on a special project. "One year she put in a pond; another year new cabinets. Once she put in a nice brick sidewalk and was really looking forward to my reaction—but I walked right over it without noticing."

RAGBRAI helped drive another couple apart. "My husband got addicted to RAGBRAI," says the now-divorced woman, who prefers not to be named. "All of his training, going to RAGBRAI meetings, making gift boxes…you name it, plus all of the time away during the ride, itself, robbed our family of some valuable quality time.

"I biked with him one day of RAGBRAI, and we camped together, but I was not wowed by it, like he was," she adds. "One summer we were going to go to Europe, but as soon as they announced the RAGBRAI route, he started pouting. Long story short, we didn't go to Europe, and RAGBRAI contributed to our breakup."

BANTER

One thing RAGBRAI riders seem to share is a propensity to chat while cycling, waiting in line or sitting in bars. I've overheard conversations about everything from saddle sores, which I won't repeat, to translational genomics, which I couldn't repeat.

Iowa has some of the world's biggest wind farms.

I've heard discouraging words ("This is worse than anything Outward Bound ever threw at me"), as well as encouraging words ("It don't get no gooder than this"). To "slowing" and "stopping," verbal signals that riders share, a guy added "sweating!" That prompted a gal to add "dying!"

One man said to his companion, "Slow down, I want to catch this punch line." I went back and asked to hear the joke. It goes like this: A RAGBRAI cyclist walks into a bar and orders a drink. The bartender says, "You're really sweaty. What have you been doing?" The rider answers, "Sitting on my ass all day."

RAGBRAI chatter could be grist for novelists and screenwriters. Here are a few choice snippets:
- Passing huge wind turbines: "Look, someone put up a bunch of big fans to keep us cool."
- "Wow! I never knew they even made this many bikes!"
- "Look at that hawk, circling overhead."
    "Yeah, don't slow down!"
- "The next time anyone tells you that Iowa is flat, you have my permission to punch them in the face," to which someone chimed in, "You know what I always say. 'Where there's a hill, there's a way.'"
- "Would ya look at that? Who says no one looks good in spandex!"
- "I did Monday. They can never take that away from me."
- A father to his young son, as they passed a large hog confinement lot, "It's going to smell like that the whole way, and I don't want to hear another word about it."
- "Uuugh. Why did they build Cedar Rapids so far away [eighty-five miles] from Marshalltown [the next overnight town]?"
- "This ride is making me realize what an incredible machine the bicycle is."
    "You want incredible? How about my body…holding up to all this abuse!"

Art

Merita Guthrie of Fort Dodge finds inspiration in RAGBRAI for her artistic talents. She began creating bike art in 1986, airbrushing T-shirts sold on RAGBRAI through Irwin's Bike and Sports. Because each shirt was individually painted by hand, she made only about twenty that year. Since then, her business has grown to two hundred to three hundred T-shirts a year, now sold on RAGBRAI through Bikes to You, a shop in Grinnell.

Some of her T-shirts are licensed to say "RAGBRAI," but others just celebrate Iowa and biking. "With my RAGBRAI designs, I always include a pig, a barn, some corn and a bike," she says. Why? "Because people like them. Also, with a pig, I don't have to worry about portraying the gender, race, ethnicity or anything else. I want my shirts to be fun for everyone."

Guthrie's designs are usually playful and colorful. She applies the designs to postcards and posters, as well as T-shirts, and sells them under the brand name Tour

Merita Guthrie created this playful design to celebrate RAGBRAI XXXV. *Merita Guthrie, Tour de Farms.*

de Farms. She does two RAGBRAI designs a year, one day and one night scene, but always in a limited quantity, numbered and signed.

While Guthrie does art year round, she also works in an elementary school, which gives her the summer to produce her designs and do RAGBRAI.

Sleeping in a tent at night and selling T-shirts and postcards all day is sometimes tiring for her and her husband, Dwight. Nevertheless, Guthrie loves RAGBRAI. "The people are awesome, with a capital AWE," she says. "We have friends we see only once a year on RAGBRAI, but when we do, it's like we just had dinner with them the week before."

Signs

Part of the appeal of RAGBRAI is being off the Interstate, on smaller roads not blighted with billboards and advertisements. The signs you encounter on RAGBRAI are—like the pie—likely to be homemade. Many signs are clever, such as "Church Open. Pray and P for Free!" (presumably in that order). The most common signs welcome riders:

- Outside Battle Creek in 1988 near the end of one of RAGBRAI's toughest days ever: "You've battled the hills, now rest at the Creek."
- Outside Conrad in 1995 for cyclists who had completed RAGBRAI's century loop: "Welcome Century Loopers, from all the Century Loopers at Oakview Nursing Home."
- In Anthon in 1988: "Wall Drug: 433 miles. Anthon United Methodist Church: 0.5 miles."

Other signs are funny or silly:
- Near Belmond's kybos in 1993: "Kyboville: population 10, with waiting for 500. A little place with international appeal: You're Russian when you come and Finnish when you leave."
- Outside New York (population 5) in 1997: "Welcome to New York, Iowa—the Little Apple."
- Advertising a place to see baby chickens: "Attractive chicks ahead."
- A series of three signs along the road in 2012: "This is corn" [with an arrow]. "This is beans" [with an arrow]. "That's about it."

In 1980, flag-bedecked signs along RAGBRAI went unread by their intended target. Gary Kramer was not able to bike with his wife but didn't want her to think he had forgotten their anniversary. Therefore, he asked mayors of towns along the route to put up "happy anniversary" signs for her that day. Three towns complied, but Carol never saw them because she had quit the day before due to the hills. Or perhaps

It's a tradition on RAGBRAI not to price gouge.

she just wanted to spend their anniversary together—or return home to see if Gary remembered. Proof that he had appeared in the newspaper the next day.

GIVING BACK

When many people hear about a five-hundred-mile bike ride, they assume it's organized to raise money for some charitable cause like fighting cancer. That would make sense, but RAGBRAI doesn't have to make sense. It's a fun-raiser, not a fundraiser.

Many riders wear T-shirts that express a cause such as "I ride with diabetes" and "World Bicycle Relief," a nonprofit organization that provides rugged bicycles to people in developing countries. Still, the riders wearing them aren't typically raising money. And even though a few teams have sprung up in recent years that require members to secure donations for a cause, they have not changed RAGBRAI's casual character.

Ironically, not being wedded to one particular cause allows RAGBRAI to help hundreds of causes every year. As RAGBRAI nation crosses the state, cyclists contribute to schools, churches, booster clubs and community organizations whenever they buy food and drink from these groups. A quick look around one corner in Dows in 1978

As riders give back through their purchases and donations, RAGBRAI has funded many park benches, church roofs and fire trucks. *Ken Urban Photography.*

showed that the following groups were selling Kool Aid, doughnuts or other items: Crossroads Club, Future Farmers of America, Swimming Pool Board, Thursday Club, Liberty Club, American Legion, Jaycees and several churches. And these groups raise hundreds or thousands of dollars at a time. Sometimes, riders are motivated to make contributions, as well.

RAGBRAI itself donates money to community causes around the state. Ever since it started charging a registration fee in 1982, the organization has been donating its profits to charitable organizations and community causes. That money has paid for lots of park benches, basketball equipment, school roofs, church organs, fire trucks and, yes, band uniforms, as in Meredith Wilson's fictional River City, Iowa, made famous by *The Music Man*. In 1999, Algona used its money to fund the town's sesquicentennial; Spencer to refurbish a bike trail; Clear Lake to improve water quality; and Decorah to promote tourism.

Most teams and many individuals give back by thanking their Iowa hosts with a gift. Kaye and Carter LeBeau traditionally give a specially selected, handcrafted sculpture from Isabel Bloom Sculptures, a studio in their hometown of Davenport. "Kaye said I was an 'angel' to host them, so they sent me a sculpture of an angel," says Phyllis Lane about one of the three times she hosted them.

Dave Cooney was so impressed with how much work Iowans put into planning and organizing for the "invasion" of cyclists that he "wanted to give back" to the towns, he says. For the past eight years, he has planted a tree in every overnight and ending town while biking RAGBRAI.

Cooney volunteers with nonprofits that plant trees in Muscatine. Why not do the same thing on RAGBRAI? he asked himself. In 2005 and 2006, the Iowa Department of Natural Resources provided the trees he planted, but the following year he had to pay for them himself. Since then, the Melon City Bike Club has paid for the trees, which represents about $800 per year.

Cooney organizes the planting and does the work himself, which usually adds a couple of hours to an already long day. Digging a three-foot-deep by three-foot-round hole, preparing the soil, lifting heavy loads and watering the tree after biking seventy or eighty miles is not easy, even when he has helpers. Still, "there's never been a day that I didn't look forward to doing it," Cooney says. "So far, we've planted sixty-five trees on RAGBRAI. Now I'd like to expand the program."

SAFETY MISSION

Rich Ketcham, a software consultant, started profiling RAGBRAI's route in 1995, noting mileage and elevation. This was pretty advanced for that time, so he tried to sell the idea to RAGBRAI. It was not interested; instead, Ketcham started handing out printed copies of the ride profile each day. They were so popular that he created a website with the information and backfilled all the data to the first ride.

The result is http://www.geobike.com, a fabulous site chock-full of data about mileage, elevation, routes and host towns. Ketcham has since been able to sell this profiling service to other bike rides, but he does this for RAGBRAI on a volunteer basis. "I love Iowa and am crazy about this ride," he says.

Ketcham has accompanied RAGBRAI officials on route inspection trips, employing software he developed that uses GPS to pinpoint the location of road hazards (potholes, cracks, bad railroad crossings, loose gravel, weak shoulders, etc.) so they can be reported and fixed—or at least indicated with warning signs. "The more everyone is aware of road conditions and the ride characteristics, the safer the ride will be," he says.

OTHER RIDES

More than forty states hold big, multi-day bicycle rides, and they have all looked at or been inspired by RAGBRAI, the queen mother of cross-state bike rides. In 1979, forty-year-old Dot Moss of Pooler, Georgia, rode RAGBRAI and enjoyed it so much that she wrote to Georgia's governor and got permission to organize a bike ride across her state. Now called the Bicycle Ride Across Georgia (BRAG), the seven-day, family-friendly ride occurs in June and attracts about one thousand riders.

RAGBRAI also sparked the six-day Bicycle Ride Across Nebraska (BRAN), founded in 2000 after a Rotarian heard about RAGBRAI and suggested doing something similar in Nebraska. It attracts only about six hundred people, partly because of the long distances between towns.

The six-day, five hundred-mile Bicycle Illinois runs from Cairo to Chicago. It includes hotel stays and optional century loops every day.

The weeklong Bike Florida is quite different than RAGBRAI, says Juskiewicz, who helped develop it before becoming director of RAGBRAI. "It's smaller, more touristic, travels along the beach and occurs in the spring."

Ride the Rockies in Colorado is limited to 2,500 participants, so it can be difficult to get into. Also, it's difficult to ride. Although the total feet climbed on some RAGBRAIs has exceeded the comparable number on some Ride the Rockies, the latter is more difficult to ride because the climbing is more concentrated and the route is more challenging.

"You could climb for three hours at five miles per hour and then coast for a few minutes at forty-five miles per hour, even as the road twists and turns, with traffic," says John Becker. "Compared to RAGBRAI, you have to prepare more carefully and take more gear due to the thin air at high altitudes; long climbs; changeable weather, including severe cold and snowstorms; and the possibility of forest fires."

"Of all the rides that RAGBRAI inspired, none of them comes close to duplicating what we have in Iowa," says Mark Wyatt, executive director of the Iowa Bicycle Coalition. "Other states just don't have our network of farm-to-market roads—or Iowans!"

Chapter 11

IOWA AND RAGBRAI

A Good Fit

The land that became Iowa was part of the Louisiana Purchase from France in 1803. This is reflected in the Iowa flag, which is the French flag with the Iowa seal superimposed on the middle white stripe.

The United States acted quickly to claim and explore this land. Within one year, Meriwether Lewis and William Clark began to explore the region. As they headed up the Missouri River, they lost one member of their team when Charles Floyd died of a ruptured appendix. He was buried on a promontory point in what is now Sioux City, something that has been heralded each of the six times RAGBRAI started in that city.

In 1805, the scientifically astute President Thomas Jefferson launched another exploration, this one up the Mississippi River led by Zebulon Pike. It passed Iowa's first permanent white settlement on the west bank of the Mississippi, the home of Julien Dubuque, a French trapper who had settled there from Quebec. The city that bears his name would be a RAGBRAI ending town four times.

Thus, by exploring the burgeoning country's two greatest rivers—the two rivers that make Iowa a modern-day Mesopotamia, the two rivers that RAGBRAI links—the United States began to close in on the land that would become Iowa.

From Mighty Mo to the Big Muddy, the region gave way to Manifest Destiny. In 1808, the United States established Fort Madison on the Mississippi River to defend its interests from Native Americans and European powers. After troops abandoned the fort during the War of 1812, white settlement in the region slowed. Twenty years later, only about fifty white people lived in what is now Iowa. It was still considered Indian territory. That changed dramatically at the conclusion of the Black Hawk War in 1832, when Native Americans were removed from the region.

Jefferson's settlement theory, which was still prevalent, called for orderly development. Land was to be surveyed and divided into neat squares. Then agents and claims offices were to sell off the parcels.

Residents of Sac City in front of their history museum enjoy the parade on wheels of RAGBRAI XL.

This did not happen in the Midwest. The removal of the Indians sparked a flood of American settlers. Thousands of farmers, miners, merchants and adventurers poured into the region before the government was able to survey the land, much less establish claims offices. By 1838, twenty-three thousand settlers, technically trespassers, had taken possession of the best land in what was to become Iowa.

These early settlers were allowed to purchase the land on which they had squatted. Most of them paid only the minimum of $1.25 per acre at public auction. To discourage outsiders from bidding, the settlers appeared en masse at the claims office when their locale was being auctioned.

Over the years, many of these groups of settlers coalesced into "claims clubs," with constitutions, officers and rules stating qualifications for membership, the maximum amount of land the squatter could claim and the annual improvements he must make on his land to validate his claim.

Historians are divided on whether these claims clubs represented grassroots democracy or exploitation of the public domain for private gain. In any event, they are the first example of effective farm organization on the Iowa frontier and proved to the farmer that there was strength in collective organization, according to Joseph Wall, in his wonderful book *Iowa*. Claims clubs encouraged farmers to work together in other ways against railroads, banks, land speculators and government bodies. Eventually, this contributed to the creation of collectives and co-ops that, together with clubs, churches and civic organizations, are so strong in Iowa today and play such a central role in organizing and promoting local communities during RAGBRAI.

Iowa became a territory in 1838, with Burlington as the territorial capital, reflecting the fact that most of the action in those early days was on and along the banks of the Mississippi River. Then, in an effort to push the center of gravity farther west, the territorial government in 1841 moved the capital to Iowa City, a town created for that purpose on the banks of the Iowa River. In 1846, Iowa became a state, and in 1857, the state moved its capital still farther west to Des Moines, smack in the middle of the state. As intended, Des Moines' central location helped unite the state politically, economically and socially.

Newspapers became increasingly influential, including the *Des Moines Star*, founded in 1849. That paper evolved into the *Des Moines Register*, which would be read statewide and become very influential. If the capital had remained in Burlington, on the eastern edge of the state, or even in Iowa City, toward the eastern side of the state, it's unlikely that a newspaper published there would have had the influence, prestige or readership to spawn a statewide event such as RAGBRAI.

The land-hungry settlers kept coming, attracted by Iowa's deep, fertile soil that was being trumpeted by promoters and boosters back East. By 1850, nearly 200,000 settlers inhabited the young state. By 1860, that number had climbed to more than 600,000. Only twenty-eight years after the floodgates had opened, most of the state was settled and being farmed.

From the beginning, Iowa's settlers were bent on commercial farming. The land was so rich that it clearly supported big cash crops. The first farmers planted primarily wheat, oats, flax, fruit trees and barberry. None of these crops was native to the region, which made them vulnerable to local plant diseases. Only Indian maize, which had been cultivated in the region for centuries, was disease resistant.

By the 1880s, most Iowa farmers were planting corn, but they remained diversified. After World War II, however, they turned to the monoculture farming of corn. Later, they added soybeans, and the state rapidly became the nation's top grower of these two cash crops that so dominate the scenery on RAGBRAI.

TOWNS

As farmers settled the land, towns sprang up to serve their needs, offering stores, blacksmiths, churches, doctors, veterinarians—and a gathering place for Saturday night. These towns had to be easy for farmers to reach, so most were located a scant eight to ten miles apart. By 1910, Iowa had 838 towns, a large number for a state with only 2.2 million inhabitants.

Iowa has an inordinate number of counties. The attractive county seats, spread evenly across the state, make great host towns. *Ken Urban Photography.*

For legal, governmental and banking needs, farmers would have to travel to their county seat, a larger town with a courthouse, lawyers offices and banks. When they were being established, county seats had to be close enough for county residents to get there, conduct their business and return home by wagon within one day. Therefore, Iowa created a relatively large number of small counties, laying out ninety-nine counties in a grid-like pattern. Most counties placed their governing seats in the middle.

This large number of small towns interspersed with fewer but still many larger county seats makes Iowa ideal for a festive, cross-state bicycle ride. The small towns offer frequent places to stop, with local color and charm. The larger county seats offer more amenities and the capacity to host thousands of people overnight.

Transportation

Roads were vital to Iowa's development. They connected the state's great number of farms and towns and allowed farmers to transport their crops to market. Starting in the 1830s, primitive dirt roads crisscrossed the state. The first road with a hard surface, a wooden-plank toll road, was built in 1851. Gravel, wooden blocks, compacted earth and other materials were also experimented with.

Forward thinking about transportation, Iowa was active in the Good Roads Movement of the 1910s and 1920s. This led to many miles of roads and steadily improved roads. The completion of Iowa's first interurban concrete highway, eleven miles between Mason City and Clear Lake, was dedicated in 1918 with a ride from one town to the other by buggies, wagons, automobiles (the relative newcomer)—and decorated bicycles. Sounds a bit like RAGBRAI!

So does the River to River Road, a cross-state route that was officially designated in 1918. Running from Council Bluffs to Davenport, the route was strongly supported by the *Des Moines Register*, which saw it as a way to help unify the state and encourage commerce and tourism.

Ultimately, Iowa would have far more paved roads than other states of comparable size and population. In 2012, when its population was 3 million, Iowa had approximately 114,000 miles of state and county roads—more lane miles of highway per capita (0.077 miles) than any other state, except Kansas.

Often referred to as roads to nowhere, Iowa's farm-to-market roads have been surprisingly tenacious. A number of them have been downgraded, as Iowa's farms get bigger, its towns fade and its population ages and stagnates. Still, most of these roads are still in place and well maintained. The secondary road network is so vast that it will have no problem continuing to meet the needs of RAGBRAI and other big organized bike rides for decades to come. Recreational biking is huge in Iowa, generating $365 million a year in revenue. Governor Terry Branstad was on solid ground when he declared Iowa the bicycling capital of the nation.